Helmbrecht Breinig, Jürgen Gebhardt, Bernd

German and American Higher Education

Publikationen der Bayerischen Amerika-Akademie

Publications of the Bavarian American Academy

Band 1a

LIT

Helmbrecht Breinig, Jürgen Gebhardt,
Berndt Ostendorf (eds.)

German and American Higher Education

Educational Philosophies and Political Systems

LIT

Cover Photos: Universität München ©LMU, Pressestelle; Widener Library
©President and Fellows of Harvard College

Gedruckt auf alterungsbeständigem Werkdruckpapier entsprechend
ANSI Z3948   DIN ISO 9706

Die Deutsche Bibliothek – CIP-Einheitsaufnahme

German and American Higher Education : Educational Philosophies and Political
Systems / Helmbrecht Breinig, Jürgen Gebhardt, Berndt Ostendorf (eds.) . –
Münster : Lit, 2001
    (Publikationen der Bayerischen Amerika-Akademie/Publications of the Bavarian
    American Academy ; 1a.)
    ISBN 3-8258-4943-0

© LIT VERLAG Münster – Hamburg – London
  Grevener Str. 179   48159 Münster   Tel. 0251-23 50 91   Fax 0251-23 19 72

Distributed in North America by:

Transaction Publishers
New Brunswick (U.S.A.) and London (U.K.)

Transaction Publishers
Rutgers University
35 Berrue Circle
Piscataway, NJ 08854

Tel.: (732) 445 - 2280
Fax: (732) 445 - 3138
for orders (U. S. only):
toll free (888) 999 - 6778

CONTENTS

PREFACE

In the current debate about educational reform in Germany, the so-called "American system" of higher education frequently serves as a positive point of comparison. The relevance of U.S. institutional and organizational models is a recurrent theme in publications like *Forschung und Lehre*, the journal of the German Association of University Professors. Such scholarly contributions notwithstanding, notions of American universities, study programs, degrees, ranking, etc. often remain reductionist and stereotypical, particularly among political decision makers and journalists; even university administrators are not immune to oversimplifications.

The Bavarian American Academy (BAA), a new state institution founded with the purpose of facilitating and coordinating interdisciplinary research on North America at the various Bavarian universities, therefore devoted its first international conference to the topic "German and American Higher Education in Comparison: Educational Philosophies, Political Systems, Funding." The conference took place at the Bavarian-American Center in Munich, March 5–7, 1999. Among the subjects discussed were: basic differences between the two systems, i.e. the egalitarian German and the diversified and hierarchical American system of higher education; structure and governance of universities in both countries, in particular the role and power of state legislatures and state governments, boards, university administrations, faculties; models of costs and funding including the question of tuition; rights, duties and functions of professors and teaching staff; diversity and minority representation among faculty and students; student access, expectations and performance; and teaching vs. research, with a glance at the role of research-supporting endowments. Rather than restricting itself to a uni-directional perspective, the conference tried to answer the following questions: What are the characteristic elements of the two systems? What can they learn from each other? What parts of the system may be adopted either way?

For this purpose, the organizers brought together a large number of experts from both countries. Among the speakers were four university presidents, the president of the American Association of University Professors, a representative of the German Academic Exchange Service (DAAD), university administrators, the director of a Max-Planck Institute and the director of the European branch of the National Science Foundation as well as a number of university professors from several fields concerned with basic questions of higher education. The keynote address was delivered by Michael Heyman, Secretary of the Smithsonian Institution and ex-Chancellor of the University of California, Berkeley. All in all, 42 German and American universities were represented. The lively discussion among this highly competent group left its impact on the published versions of a number of conference papers.

The statistical data given in some of the papers are those prepared for the conference in 1999. Updates are available; they can usually be downloaded from internet sources such as those given at the end of Robert Glidden's paper.

In view of the significance of the conference proceedings for both German and American readers, the BAA decided to publish the papers in both languages, as separate volumes. I wish to thank the contributors who readily consented to have their papers included. President Kohler deserves particular gratitude for stepping in during the conference at a day's notice and for providing us with a text for publication, nonetheless. Thanks are also due to Dr. Dagmar Weiler, Stefanie Grimm, Barbara Wolfram and Dr. Ralph Poole, Dr. Stephan Fuchs and Sabine Booz for their efforts in transforming the conference from an oral into a printed event. Dr. Edward Reif and Gayle Goldstick prepared English versions for two of the texts. The Bavarian Ministry for Science, Research and the Arts generously provided the funds for the BAA and thus, too, for the conference and the publication.

"German and American Higher Education in Comparison" proved to be a highly rewarding occasion for the exchange of information and scholarly opinion. It was not the first conference of its kind: as early as 1966, the German Association for American Studies devoted its convention to the topic "American Universities and German University Reform." Nor will it be the last. Like the conference, the published volumes are supposed to continue a discussion that is beginning to be more sophisticated on both sides of the Atlantic, in accordance with Humboldt's dictum that in organizing the institutions of higher education everything depends upon the principle of "considering learning as something not yet achieved and never to be completely achieved and yet, as such, constantly to be pursued."

Erlangen, January, 2001   Helmbrecht BREINIG
                                            Director, Bavarian American Academy

INTRODUCTION:
BEYOND HUMBOLDT – AMERICA?

Jürgen GEBHARDT [1]

"Today German universities are moving within a conceptual triangle, whose vertices are marked by three phantom debates: the catastrophe of higher education, higher education for the masses, and the 'emigration' of research into areas outside the university. These phantom debates have become a chronic agenda reckoning against an uncertain background of cultural and educational politics within a federally regulated research management." [2] There is no lack of diagnoses for these crises, nor of programmatic ideas towards reform, but there is a lack on the part of society's elites to make conceptual connections between diagnoses and therapy and to arrive at a consensus over the fundamental principles, which would serve as a guide for action for a complete reform of the entire system of higher education. This is where the attempts at reform in the '60s and '70s failed. The "culture wars" over the modernization of higher education resulted in the binary and asymmetrical system of research universities (86 universities plus 7 comprehensive institutions of higher learning) and 188 colleges of applied sciences), a system hardly able to cope with the massive increase in student numbers, since each institution was bound into a corset of financial, organizational, and structural regulations set by state bureaucracies which answered to governmental authorities that in turn were colored by partisan politics. The multiplication of existing universities could not do justice to the demands made by 1.8 million students (as of winter 1998/99) upon higher education, for it took place within the legal fiction of the principle of equality among all universities. Another notion had already become illusory, namely that the concept of a graduate education in special disciplines, in the sense of a research-oriented training, could be translated into professional, i.e. job-related education for a rapidly increasing student body. "Humboldt no longer works for mass universities. Education via scholarship, the unity of research and teaching, pursuit of knowledge in solitude and freedom – all this

---

[1]   In collaboration with Helmbrecht Breinig and Berndt Ostendorf
[2]   Jürgen Mittelstraß, *Die unzeitgemäße Universität* (Frankfurt: Suhrkamp, 1994) 31.

had a chance when three or five percent of a given cohort in secondary education went on to study at university. With the current 30 percent and more, these educational precepts represent in fact no more than a myth ....."[3] Open access, an egalitarian pay scale and financial assistance ensured the stability of the system at a relatively high level up until the time when the financing of the system through public spending reached a limit which society was not willing to cross.

The university system, imperfectly adapted to the new situation and consequently overtaxed in its internal organization and overall structure, increasingly found itself in a crisis of modernization that also "involved the notion of scholarship itself and the ordering of knowledge into disciplines and subjects," as Mittelstraß puts it.[4] But if a university is not able to formulate a reflexive notion of its own purpose, it will not be in any position to present society with standards of measure for the conceptual modernization of the system of higher education. Michael Daxner in 1993 listed the various discourses of crisis and modernization, that are in themselves heterogeneous, as follows:

a) There is a lack of societal consensus over what place institutes of higher learning should occupy in the hierarchy of political and social importance and hence in the allocation of finances. This depends on political priorities, on the willingness to allocate funds, on the direction and nature of reforms and developments and, not least of all, on the definition of what is crucial in higher education.

b) Chronic under-financing with its immediate and long-term consequences determines the structure of the discourse in higher education to the detriment of the discussion of content.

c) The dissolution of ties within institutions of higher learning and thus the decrease in institutional loyalty and a willingness to contribute are indeed recognized passively, but not actively thematized.

d) The lack of clear goals regarding the functions of scholarly education, professional preparation, and training in the changed coordinates of power in the nation, Europe, and in the global standard provoke incompetent decisions and practical uncertainty regarding the levels of responsibility.[5]

It was not least of all under the pressure of empty coffers that a restructuring process began within higher education and the sciences in which the divergent positions of politicians, the bureaucrats administering scholarship, the makers of public opinion, and not least of all the managers of big companies found their expression. Under the pretext of reform, the system of higher education

---

[3]   Mittelstraß 26.
[4]   Mittelstraß 56.
[5]   Michael Daxner, *Die Wiederherstellung der Hochschule* (Cologne: Heinrich Böll Stiftung, 1993).

is undergoing a restructuring by federal and state legislatures which is characterized by mutually exclusive objectives and corresponding partial changes – without any consideration of the structural and functional overall coherence of the system of an institution of higher learning as a political and cultural agent of socialization and as a locus of rationally-based knowledge of availability and orientatie, which is to say as a source of the material, intellectual, and cultural welfare of the society.

"In reforming higher education, everyone wants to do as he pleases," Kurt Reumann quite rightly commented recently in the *FAZ*. And thus piecemeal engineering takes its course and cures individual symptoms but lacks a guiding principle. Thus, no new vision of academia has been emerging from the intellectual creativity and the impulse for reform of the professorate and its representatives. Equally deficient is the communication to the society at large, notwithstanding the interesting contributions of individuals such as Daxner, Glotz[6], Mittelstraß or Michael Greven[7], and not to mention those of higher education politics in the program papers of the *Wissenschaftsrat* (scholarship advisory board) and the committees of the cultural ministers and rectors. The collective inability to put through reforms "expresses itself in various ways, among which is that the university perceives itself to be an educational institution in which a state of emergency is the rule, the will to change is weak, and the loyalty of the teachers, students, and researchers for their institution of higher learning is hardly discernible."[8] These words – presented in Erlangen in 1993 – no longer fully describe the present state in higher education. They do continue to be valid, however, in as far as the gridlock of the collegiate bodies of academic self-administration has not been broken yet and there is a lack of programmatically consistent and conceptionally well thought out collective action. But the universities were forced into action by the government's higher education policy, and a flurry of intra-university reform activities began. This is not to say that the interplay of governmental higher education policy and intra-university reorganization of teaching and research do not achieve goals that are in themselves completely sensible, but it does not go beyond "the juxtaposition and pluralism of different interests and perspectives which resembles a concert

---

[6]   Peter Glotz, *Im Kern verrottet? Fünf vor zwölf an Deutschlands Universitäten* (Stuttgart: Deutsche Verlagsanstalt, 1996).

[7]   Michael Greven, "Universitätskrise und Universitätspolitik in Zeiten populistischer Demokratie," *Politik und Politea*, ed. Wolfgang Leibhold (Würzburg: Könighausen& Neumann, 2000) 267-285.

[8]   Mittelstraß 13.

of sparrows", [9] which is determined by the piecemeal engineering of the policy of higher education reform on the whole induced by the government and political parties. Just as ever before, this is based on the premise that the existing binary system of higher education is expected in principle to form the framework for all efforts at reform – a uniform system, financed and regulated by the government, which nonetheless allows for local modifications insured by experimentation clauses. In reality, however, the reform strategies as a whole are moving toward a fundamental change in the system in one decisive point: the tendency toward the elimination of the constituent corporate structural principle of academic self-government, which is constitutive for the German university idea. The reform favors the hierarchical structural principle which was originally subordinated to the first. The move towards management sciences is giving the idea of self-administrating autonomy a new meaning through the strengthening of leadership positions of rectors, chancellors and deans recently introduced in connection with boards of an external council (*Hochschulrat*). On the one hand, the autonomy of institutions of higher education vis-à-vis government authorities is being strengthened by greater self-determination in fiscal and budgetary matters. At the same time the rights of collegiate bodies of the university and especially of the professorate are diminished. Such a development may be sensible in terms of higher education and research policy, but what is astounding about it is that this change in the system is not thematized in a fundamental discussion, neither in public nor in the representative bodies of the professors, or even in the ministries and parliamentary committees.

On the one hand, this marks the conceptual impotence of the German discussion, but on the other hand, it explains the omnipresent conceptual recourse to internationally successful models of reform. This means – aside from rather marginal consideration of Dutch or Scandinavian models of reform – for the most part a conceptual orientation on the Anglo-Saxon and here especially on the American system of higher education. Politics, public opinion, the bureaucratic administration of scholarship, business, and not least of all the university elites themselves all operate under the impression of success in terms of scientific performance and economic efficiency of an educational system well adapted for the professional preparation of the masses in a free democratic society.

It naturally follows that this system implicitly and explicitly is the model for reform programs on the whole and for sector-related structural reforms of the system of higher education as they concern university organization: the

---

[9]   Greven 266.

reorganization of the scholarly disciplines, the requirements for the fields of study and examinations, the pay scales for staff, the promotion of research, etc. This is proven by:

- the introduction of higher education supervisory councils (*Hochschulrat*) modeled upon the American boards of trustees,
- the strengthening of senior administrators following the model of presidents and deans,
- the professionalization of the administration,
- the organization of the disciplines or chairs into departments,
- pay commensurate with performance and the allocation of research funding on the basis of an evaluation by senior administrators or peers of the effectiveness of research and teaching activities of departmental units and professors,
- student evaluations,
- establishment of junior professors and the doing away with the *Habilitation*,
- the drafting of programs of studies leading to Bachelor's and Master's degrees (partly taught in English),
- government support of private institutions of higher learning outside of and to the detriment of the state institutions and
- the promotion of university-related private enterprises that commercialize and market the results of academic research.

Looking at the present politics of reform under the aspect of the reception of American role models, the question naturally arises to what extent this reception is based upon proper perception. Beyond that, it is necessary to ask whether the aim of modernizing German institutions of higher learning can be achieved through the intended transfer of ideas and institutions. In other words, what are the requirements for a successful conceptual synthesis (at least in some areas) of two societal models of academic institutions that differ strongly in their sociopolitical and cultural assumptions? Or, as an alternative to such a synthesis, to what extent should specifically American component parts be integrated into the restructuring of German higher education?

As a rule, such questions are not raised in German reform discussions, for the exemplary nature of the American university appears to be self-evident in the limited perceptions of the German public: in the light of this perception, Harvard, Stanford, or Yale are everywhere.

To begin with, it should be emphasized that, seen globally, educational and research institutions are to a large extent a hybrid product of transfer and transplantation processes. In the final analysis, then, even the ideal type of American research university is a reformed institution modeled after the German university of the 19*th* century and as such is a German-American hybrid. Moreover, it must be pointed out that, in contrast to the uniform structure of corporations under public law which determines the German setting, the scene in America is characterized by an almost inestimable spectrum of variation and institutional diversification in terms of ways of control and internal setup, statement of purpose and system capability of the "institutions of higher learning." It is consequently impossible to take the leading research universities as an ideal type and to derive from them definite model conceptions. Even in a simple institutional comparison without taking the context into account, one is in danger of comparing "apples and oranges" and reaching the wrong conclusions.

In a position statement for the German Association of Scholars of English (*Deutscher Anglistenverband*), Stephan Kohl, Monika Fludernik, and Hubert Zapf have already drawn attention to the difficulty of making such comparisons and, under the title "Vorbild Amerika?" ("America as a Model?") have listed and refuted ten current erroneous notions. [10] The authors' findings are instructive. But they argue from the perspective of the humanities, and they leave out for the most part the connections to the politics of higher education and research. They also insist in a somewhat idealizing manner upon the status quo of the German university, whose problems they almost only see in a lack of budgetary support. Despite these reservations, it must be stated that Kohl and his colleagues have shown numerous misconceptions about the actual state of affairs in American academia and have refuted claims based upon them.

An enlightening discourse on the prerequisites for the possibility of a transatlantic synthesis requires a dialogue between Germans and Americans who have proven to be experts on the subject. This should ideally combine a systemic analysis with detailed studies in such a way that well-considered judgements of a synthesis's reform potential become possible, even if it is

---

[10] The authors refer to the following – to their minds incorrect – assumptions: 1. "American universities are better." 2. "German universities must allow themselves to be compared with leading universities in North America." 3. "American and German degrees are comparable to each other." 4. "Education takes longer at German universities than it does at American universities." 5. "American students work harder than Germans students do." 6. "American professors work harder than German professors do." 7. "Cost neutral reforms to German universities following the American model are possible." 8. "In contrast to American universities, German universities know no criteria for judging achievement." 9. "In America, teaching evaluations have a decisive influence on professors' careers." 10. "In contrast to American universities, German universities are not internationally attractive." Cf. Kohl et al., "Vorbild Amerika?" <http://www.anglistenverband.de/amerika.html>. A shortened version can be found in *Forschung & Lehre* 6 (2000): 302-305.

restricted to specific sectors. The Bavarian-American Academy conference whose proceedings are published in this volume provided the occasion for such a dialogue. It was intended was not merely to present a "thick description" of the academic worlds in which the problem areas are explored, but also to provide the German reform discussion with a mode of reflection which it is especially lacking in its recourse to the American model. Even if the meeting did not succeed in surveying the entire field in the desired manner, a sufficient number of findings were made to allow for a discussion of the American university's function as a model with a view toward the problem areas that are to be discussed here and now. In the following, some relevant complexes of questions will be presented in the brevity called for.

1. Who receives what kind of higher education in what institutional form?

The binary German system of research universities and colleges for applied sciences (to which have to be added the conservatories, the art colleges and several special academies plus the newest "private" institutions of higher learning) which 1.8 million students are currently availing themselves of, is institutionally standardized, government controlled, and uniform in its legal status, the structure of its organization and the categorization of the staff as well as the academic programs of study. It stands in contrast to a highly diverse American system of state, private, and commercial institutions with various educational missions, programs of study, and degrees serving 14.9 million students. [11] Seen from a comparative viewpoint, and taking into account the quality criteria of the so-called Carnegie classification and the legal form of the administration of higher education, the diversification of higher education can be presented as follows (here the reader should be made aware that within these categories, there is yet again an internal diversification with many variants to note, which shall be overlooked here):

The public institution of higher learning is the predominant form, attended by 80 % of all students; the remaining 20 % study at private institutions of higher learning.

a) Approximately 36 % of all students covered in the statistics attended two-year community colleges or at least technical colleges. Their quality hardly

---

[11] Cf. Daniel Fallon, "Differentiation by Role and Mission of Institutions of Higher Education in the United States"; and Robert Glidden, "Mobility and Service: The Dual Role of Higher Education in U.S. Society," in this volume. Furthermore: National Center for Education Statistics, ed., *Digest of Education Statistics* (Washington: U.S. Department of Education, 1998) <http://nces.ed.gov/pubs/digest97/listtables.html>.

even corresponds to that of the last two years of German high school (*Gymnasium*) or German advanced technical schools (*Fachoberschule*).

b) The vast majority (nearly 50 %) of students are enrolled in four or five-year general liberal arts programs or specialized programs emphasizing one field such as business or engineering: teaching is based on scholarship, but not directed at scholarly specialization or research. The B.A. undergraduate program of studies is offered by all colleges classified as such and all of the following institutions in the Carnegie classification with

c) Graduate studies which are "fully academic" in the German sense of the Humboldtian model, meaning that they integrate research and education. These are distinguished in turn by the kind of degree (Masters or doctorate) and by the disciplines in which these degrees can be attained. 125 institutions of higher education have qualified as research universities. This means the right to award doctoral degrees in most (not in all) disciplines, first-class research, and appropriation of extensive federal funding. Approximately 15 % of students (2.04 million) are registered in the academic graduate programs leading to Masters, doctoral, or professional degrees (in law, medicine, veterinary medicine, and theology). This number can be compared – at least according to formal quality criteria – to 67 % of German students in equivalent educational programs. This is a number which will need to be put in perspective with regard to the scholastic quality of instructors and research, especially in terms of an intense scholarly training on the one hand and the emphasis on practical skills in the professional schools (law, medicine, etc.) on the other hand.

d) The differentiation of the various kinds of academic education manifests itself in the age of the students. At institutions of higher learning with high entrance requirements, the 18 to 22-year-olds still make up the majority of the undergraduates; looking at the entirety of Bachelor education, however, approximately 50 % are older than 22, and approximately 25 % are older than 30. The average age in the graduate schools corresponds to the German one: approximately 28 years. The majority of students is between 22 and 34 years old. The mean age for receiving a doctorate is around 33.8 years. The changes in age statistics result from the combination of studying and working: 40 % of Bachelor students are part-time students. Many return to higher education at an advanced age to gain further qualifications. This is also true for graduate studies. [12] Furthermore, the diversity in quality manifests itself in the dropout rates in the Bachelor program of study: it is low at the highly selective leading

---

[12]   Cf. especially Louis Menand, "Everybody Else's College Education," *New York Times Magazine*, 20 April 1997: 48-49.

universities (3-8 %), it corresponds to the German average at good state universities with low admissions requirements for state residents: (approximately 35 %), and it reaches 50 % and more at institutions with lesser academic reputations. As the graduation rates at NCAA Division I institutions prove, the average dropout rate is 43 %. [13]

e) An American institution of higher education always charges its students: Public institutions derive 18% and private institutions 41% of their revenue from tuition and fees. This is reflected by the range of charges for instruction: from $1200 per year at a community college up to $20,000 and more for a Bachelor program of studies at leading private universities (Harvard, Stanford). On the average, state colleges charge $2,900 for a B.A. program and private colleges charge $18,000. However, 41 % of the students at state colleges and 60 % of those at private colleges receive financial aid through full or partial scholarships. It is true for all institutions, but especially for the graduate and professional schools, that "high achievers," outstanding high school graduates and undergraduates, can study at their choice of institutions of higher learning thanks to a tightly woven net of institutional programs whose purpose it is to promote the gifted, as well as to intensive recruiting efforts on the part of individual institutions of higher learning. In general, however, the socioeconomic profile of the student body in the individual classes of the institutions reflects the social, ethnic, and regional structure of American society. The research universities are predominantly institutions for the white upper and middle-classes, and recently also increasingly for Asian Americans. [14] A system of reciprocal competition arises in so far as the individual institution of higher learning is the master over the selection of students, and these in turn apply to colleges based upon the results of their college entrance tests. In this respect, a homogeneous, motivated, and above-average student body does indeed result at the very good and good state and private institutions of higher learning. The motivation to achieve, alongside success and the best future prospects, is not least of all the financial aspect of the charges or the scholarships. Conversely, the high opinion that especially paying B.A. students have of themselves leads increasingly to the expectation that they receive excellent grades, regardless of their current state of knowledge. The student body profile at lower-ranked institutions down

---

[13] The National Collegiate Athletic Association is required by federal law to keep statistics on the graduation rates of all B.A. students of the 305 associated institutions of higher learning.

[14] Cf. C. Aisha Blackshire-Belay, "Diversifying the Pool of Faculty, Staff and Students in the Academic Setting: Who Benefits and Why?" in this volume; and Iring Wasser, *Bildung und Demokratie - Bundesstaatliche Strategien zur Förderung der Chancengleichheit im amerikanischen Bildungswesen* (Hamburg: Kovács, 1997): 197 ff.

to the community colleges reflects the decreasing criteria for admission and finds expression in the climbing dropout rates. And thus the diversified system of higher education, unlike in Germany, leads to a social pre-determination of one's chances in life, since these are directly connected to the reputation of the institution of higher learning that one attends.

In considering the advantages and disadvantages of such a diversified system of education, one will be able to make a few careful conclusions. [15] A number of factors speak in favor of diversifying higher education. On the one hand, the job market is demanding a stronger diversification – one which is based on scientific training but work oriented; on the other hand, the students think along the same lines. The German system's binary structure does not do this sufficient justice. As was noted at the beginning, it is self-deluding to assume that 67 % of German students receive a profound and broad education based on a genuine scientific training. As a rule, mass universities offer instructions in special disciplines with great latitude in electives and a heavy emphasis in the final exam. The success of the colleges for applied sciences (28 % of all students) and the demand for new programs of study at the universities speak in favor of a predominant interest in professionally oriented curricula. A further diversification through increasing the number of colleges for applied sciences and the introduction of special institutions of higher learning is one way in this direction. This is happening today in fact through the specialized institution of higher learning (supported by public funds) with technical or economic emphases and without research requirements. The other way is likewise being pursued relatively haphazardly by the universities with the introduction of professionally oriented and short-cut programs of study. But: can this balancing act between the old-style research universities and practical, professionally oriented institutions be maintained in a matter appropriate for the system? This leads to the question of how valuable is the currently pursued introduction of Bachelor's and Masters's courses of study following the Anglo-Saxon model. It is obvious that it is not the American system of undergraduate liberal education and its completely different structure which is an issue, but rather an imitation of the discipline-centered British Bachelor. Thus the conceptions oscillate between, on the one hand, a degree after three years, which is supposed to qualify the student for a profession and is at the same time designed for further qualifications toward the Master's and doctorate, and on the other hand an independently organized professionally oriented program of study. A third

---

[15]   Cf. I. Michael Heyman, "Observations on American Higher Education: Is the American System Relevant for Germany?" in this volume.

variant calls for a course of study for wealthy foreigners not open to residents. "For this reason," Michael Greven writes, "the current introduction of 'progressive programs of study with international degrees' at German universities amounts to a juggling act which, though it may not be desired politically, is nevertheless accepted .... It will hardly change anything in the essential elements of liberal arts and social science studies in Germany." [16] It must be added that with the necessary allowances this applies also to the proposed changes in the natural sciences and technical disciplines. It will require considerable money in personnel and materials to build up a conceptually well thought out Bachelor program, which contradicts the declared intention of saving money with short-cut courses of study. It also must be added that, unlike private business, the government's regulations governing career paths still do not accept a diploma from a college for applied sciences, nor the B.A. as an "academic" degree. The problem of progressive courses of study is thus inseparably connected to the issue of the diversification of higher education itself and cannot satisfactorily be solved within the existing system.

There is little sympathy in the USA, more influenced as it is by the logic of the market, for free access to tertiary education which is also free of charge. For the most part, there is also agreement in Germany over the necessity for a measured and balanced tuition. Once again, it proceeds in keeping with the spirit of piecemeal engineering. At the outset there is the intellectually dishonest decision of politicians partly to finance private institutions because they embrace reforms, which is to say: to do with charges and selective admissions what state institutions of higher education are not allowed to do. An institution of higher education's right to select its students according to aptitude would introduce an aspect of competition for good students into the game which, in spite of the students' regional immobility, would initiate diversification in the entire system and in the individual institutions of higher learning. That means open access at an affordable price for everyone willing to study, but at the desired university or in the desired field of study only in accordance with the particular entry restrictions (*numerus clausus*). To all this a caveat must be added. Even diversified education does not free teachers from the responsibility of "scholarly norms and achievement standards related to education" (Greven); the latter must include an aspect indispensable for democratic mass education, which is to make students conscious of their responsibilities as citizens for

---

[16] Greven 283; cf. also Horst Mewes, "American Higher Education: A Model for Germany? A Skeptical Perspective" in this volume.

what they do. The Humboldtian ideal of scholarship as personality formation lacks precisely this socio-ethical raison d'être of a democratic education.

Let us close this examination with one last note: with its comprehensive social services (from swimming pools to churches), the American campus traditionally represents a certain societal universe with which a student can identify in a manner unknown in Germany. An alumnus remains attached to his institution of higher learning for life (with corresponding social and financial consequences). It remains to be seen whether and to what extent corresponding attempts will be successful to form an alumni society in the face of a lack of a university infrastructure in the American sense.

2. What does the diversification of the higher education system achieve for the quality of scholarship, and what prerequisites are there for a system of high achievement at the university?

a) However an institution of higher learning is organized, the quality of its research and teaching stands or falls with the quality of the instructors. In comparison to the German universities, with their governmental regulations of pay, position, status, etc. and a relatively fixed staff structure (tenured civil service status for professors C3/C4, tenure and temporary contracts for those in middle positions, part-time faculty such as language instructors, freelance teachers), the staff structure in the USA appears to be not only more flexible, but also comparatively more achievement-oriented and consequently fairer in rewarding achievement, and on the whole appears to function more effectively. [17] The formal structure (assistant professor, associate professor, full professor) with a corresponding gradation in pay is uniform throughout the system. The salary level of an individual professor, however, reflects the diversification of the system. Depending upon the institution (and region), the salaries differ extraordinarily, just as they do within the institution depending on the field of study that the faculty member represents. The average salary for a full professor for nine months (faculty members at institutions of higher learning have three months at their disposal) at a community college amounts to $53,000 (1996/97) – at a public college it is $70,000, and at a public research University it is $72,000. The corresponding scale for private institutions is $38,000, $76,000, and $88,000. These average values do not say much about the salary differences from discipline to discipline or from individual to individual; they

---

[17] Cf. Jürgen Kohler, "Teaching vs. Research and (Part-of) Lifetime Faculty at German Universities", in this volume.

add up to be tens of thousands of dollars. The salary can be freely negotiated and is determined by supply and demand; the reputation of the applicants' alma mater is a decisive criterion here. The final decision on employment lies only to a certain extent in the hands of the professors themselves, being subject to administrative decision-making authorities.

If we make cautious comparisons, the administration at an institution of higher education can assume the role of the German ministerial bureaucracy. Three decisive aspects of the American system's staff structure must be stressed, for they are hotly debated in the German discussion:

The assistant professor, who as a rule has just finished a doctorate, receives an independent position but is dependent upon the approval of his department and the good will of his colleagues for contract extensions, promotion and tenure, and thus his advancement. This applies just as much for the promotion to a higher professorial rank, which, in contrast to Germany is customary. The primary criteria for this, just as for the pronounced pay raises which take effect at regular intervals, are the individually attributable scholarly achievements (primarily publications and the presentation of scholarship at conferences, citations, research grants, etc.) and the students' teacher evaluations based upon variously structured questionnaires. [18] Employing the instrument of the teacher evaluation contributes to avoiding obviously deplorable states of affairs in teaching. (But here the different context of the American model must be noted: the student either pays or receives a scholarship, is bound into a regimented curriculum and his academic advancement is dependent upon regular attendance and the successful completion of the course. In this way students are given incentives for learning which are not present at German universities at the moment, especially in the freely organized liberal arts and social sciences). Incidentally, pay raises associated with achievement do not end with an appointment as a full professor; he can qualify for so-called endowed chairs, which are usually named after their sponsor and are paid for by the interest of the endowment. Consequently, quality assurance at an institution of higher learning is also immediately dependent upon the allocation of funds in paying faculty members and is subject to market laws within certain boundaries. What is true for the pay scale is also true for the teaching load: it is more flexibly structured. 60 % of faculty members at a top research university teach – de-

---

[18]   Cf. a case study: J. Clifford Fox and Scott Keeter, "Improving Teaching and Its Evaluation: A Survey of Political Science Departments," *Political Science and Politics* 29.2 (1996): 174, 180.

pending on the subject – 3 to 6 hours, while 10 to 15 hours are common at a two-year state college. The same is true for the distribution of research funding and the assignment of teaching assistants etc.

Establishing assistant professors, reducing or abolishing the rank of assistants assigned to professors and the *Habilitation* (post doctoral lecturing qualification), as they are discussed in Germany, are two-edged measures, for with them, important career path motivations will become inapplicable. The American Assistant Professor is more independent personally, but as a rule he/she does not have tenure and depends on temporary contracts. Alongside a heavy teaching load, he/she is forced to produce scholarly publications after the doctorate, an equivalent to the German post doctoral *Habilitation* which, as a formal procedure, could indeed be dispensed with. If one looks at typical American career paths, professors in the lower ranks are younger (22 % are under 39); by the time they get appointed as full professors, however, the age statistics increasingly resemble those in Germany. In the relatively egalitarian German higher education system, the bonus lies in reaching the final status of the C4 professor and a relatively equal provision for staff and research funding, and the differences in quality between individual professors do not find immediate expression in a different ranking of the institutions of higher learning. [19] In the competitive American system, on the other hand, a good professor is also an expensive professor. For this reason, financial bottlenecks lead in increasing measure to cuts that reduce quality, even at medium-sized research universities and especially at lower ranked institutions: assistant professors are let go at the end of their contracts and are compensated for by new untenured staff. Tenure-track positions are no longer filled by full-time faculty, but are increasingly being replaced by part-time adjunct professors paid by the course, today, nearly 50 % of the courses at institutions of higher learning are conducted by part-time professors. It may be rightfully asserted that the long-term monitoring of students by faculty members marks the high quality of US-education, when enrollment figures match full-time faculty. Institutions that rely on an increasing number of underpaid adjunct professors can no longer maintain their standards of mentorship in the customary scope. [20] It follows for the German reform discourse that a merit-based pay scale cannot in principal be arrived at

---

[19]   Cf. Jürgen Kohler, "Teaching vs. Research and (Part-of) Lifetime Faculty at German Universities," in this volume.

[20]   Cf. Linda Perlstein, "Can Adjuncts do the Job?" *International Herald Tribune* 15 Feb. 1999: 11, 16, and James Perley, "The Position of Part-Time Adjunct vs. Full Time Faculty and the Role of AAUP," in this volume.

just by lowering the beginning salary and adding fixed financial bonuses calculated down to the penny in order to provide sufficient incentives for choosing a professorial career and compete successfully for the nation's talents (especially for the women, who have been disadvantaged up to now [21]). A pay scale that is based on academic performance of the individual scholars presupposes a system of higher education differentiated in terms of standards of excellence that sets the benchmark for the payment of the faculty member, it being a matter of negotiation. A good professor costs more than one is willing to pay to date.

b) In the face of skyrocketing costs for the maintenance of a "university of excellence," American experts unanimously argue that German society will not be in the position to support 85 research universities over a longer period of time. This statement implies the premise that German universities would like to remain internationally competitive. The question of diversification of German higher education is, therefore, not only relevant for the education of students. Instead, it is much more an issue of to what extent German scholarship can set itself off internationally. Even though the international reputation of German research is by no means as poor as the university's critics would have us believe, it is indeed correct that scholarly excellence in teaching and research in terms of international standards can only be maintained by those institutions whose role and mission is bound to this imperative.

Properly understood, international excellence means not only cutting-edge contributions to the pure and applied sciences, but also to contribute to the cultural self-understanding of a global world by means of the interpretive knowledge. For it is often overlooked that today, international intellectual and political discourses are dominated by ideas, concepts and semantics originating from academia. Thus the scholarly products of leading American universities define for the global intelligentsia the intellectual and cultural coordinates in politics, business, and culture.

The advancement of top-role universities of international caliber in Germany presupposes a diversification of the higher education system. This is the direction in which Jürgen Mittelstraß is arguing when he calls for "the consistent complementation of the university system with a competitive system of colleges for the applied sciences." The introduction of the "college for applied sciences as the standard institution of higher learning" is necessary, he says,

---

[21] Cf. Silvia Mergenthal, "Women at German Universities: a Case of Non-Diversification", in this volume.

in order that the universities once again "be able to achieve a disciplinary and competitive profile" as scholarly institutions of higher learning in a narrower sense. [22] As reasonable as this conceptually stringent suggestion is in view of the American model, its realization would mean a systemic change in German higher education that could hardly be put into practice.

Peter Glotz opposes what is in his opinion an impossible total reform with a so to speak "softer" variation on the diversification thesis: "We need institutions of higher learning that are autonomous, ones that can develop their own profile, can enter into competition with each other on the basis of these profiles and whose achievements can be made checkable in order that they be able to fulfill their duty to be accountable to society." [23] It is an open question whether and to what extent top-rate institutions will arise, claiming scholarly superiority among the German universities. A prerequisite for that would necessarily have to be a decision in favor of a specific role and mission and the organizational and qualitative restructuring of the respective institutions.

ba) The primary educational task is the strictly scholarship-oriented instruction of the entire personnel active in a growing area of research and development in an expanding educational system. Unlike in the USA, the task is to maintain the academic qualification of the teachers in the primary and secondary educational sector. An obvious weakness of the American system with corresponding consequences for the recruitment of high achievers in the disciplines of mathematics and the natural sciences reveals itself in the miserable condition of public schools in the US, thanks not least of all to the poor pay and education of their faculty. Therefore, according to the most recent findings, 60 % of the authors of the most frequently cited papers in the physical disciplines who are working in the USA were born abroad; in the life sciences they make up almost 30 %. 25 % of the founders of university-initiated biotechnological companies come from foreign countries as well – the countries of origin are first and foremost Great Britain and Germany. In these areas, Asian Americans and immigrants from Asia play an equally important role. [24]

bb) An internationally competitive profiling assumes a concentration of scientific expertise and research in departments or institutes not only in the natural and technical sciences and medicine, where this is already at least in part underway, but also in the liberal arts and social science disciplines; it also assumes interdisciplinary integration. Spreading small institutes across 86 uni-

---

[22]   Mittelstraß 17-18.
[23]   Glotz 106, also Daxner 95.
[24]   Cf. "Alien Scientists take over USA", *The Economist* 21 Aug. 1999.

versities, especially in those disciplines named last, prevents the ability to compete internationally. That is not a plea for sheer size, but rather for the provision of a qualitative 'critical mass' whose synergistic effects show up in the leading positions of big departments in American rankings.

bc) In the US, basic research at least is still concentrated at the research universities. In the opinion of many experts, relocating basic research to larger extramural research facilities proved to be harmful for university research in particular and for research in general. Returning publicly funded basic research to the university must be included in the reform discourse's catalog of objectives. [25]

3. Who governs institutions of higher education, and who funds them to what extent?

The German institution as a corporation of public law with a corporate self administration is a public institution under the jurisdiction of the department minister of the respective state government who is responsible to the parliament. Even strengthening the autonomy by delegating to the institution of higher learning decision-making powers over budgetary, staff, structure and study-related matters will change nothing in its legal position. The silent structural change in the system mentioned above is part of the strategy to relocate the powers of governance from the collegiate bodies to the top management, the deans and presidents linked up with the external councils (*Hochschulrat*). [26]

a) The American-style *board of trustees* served as a model for the recently presented semi-governmental agency of these supervisory boards, appointed by the state government and whose jurisdiction includes budgetary and structural issues. But the American system of boards varies depending upon the type of institution of higher learning. It is in regard to the respective types of regime that the distinction between "private" and "public" has a bearing.

aa) The endowment university (for example Duke University) is a private corporation. As a rule, it is governed by a board of trustees. It is filled by self recruitment. Its members are predominantly respected donors, representatives of public life, and alumni. The committee makes all final decisions in budgetary and financial matters, reaches decisions regarding programs, structure, and staff, is responsible for securing funds, and names the president, who is

---

[25] Cf. David E. Schindel, "The American Academic Marketplace," in this volume.

[26] In the following cf. Alan Geiger, "Governance and Funding of Universities in the United States," and Hans Weiler, "Changing Patterns of Governance and Finance in German Higher Education," in this volume.

responsible for management. This distribution of powers applies to all boards regardless of any other differences.

ab) The board of a church-affiliated university (e.g. Brigham Young) is made up of representatives of the sponsoring church or order and respective lay persons, also for the most part businessmen and women. Depending upon the moral strictness of the denomination, these boards also influence the moral life of the institution of higher learning.

ac) State universities are supervised by the state in question. There are consequently correspondingly different constructions of the board system. For the most part, the entire system of higher learning in an individual state is finally managed by a board of regents (the names may differ). Its members are often appointed by the governor for political reasons or (for example in Colorado) are voted in by the electorate in general elections. There may also be supplementary boards named by the governor for an individual campus. All of these boards answer to the governor and the state legislature that provide the financial support. From this necessarily results a close reciprocal relationship between an institution of higher learning and politics, out of which a pronounced institutionalized higher education lobby has developed; a strategy that German state conferences of university presidents have not yet learned, to their disadvantage. The American regime of the boards is characterized not only by the crossover between institutions of higher learning and society, but also subordinates the higher education system itself to the logic of societal processes, since it must assert itself permanently in a dynamic field of tension determined by the imperatives of education and scholarship on the one hand and the imperatives of politics and economics on the other.

Whereas in Germany the expanding jurisdiction of the university administration (with or without the supervisory council) has not (yet) affected the election of the administrative offices by the collegiate bodies, and the professors' rights to freedom are insured by the Constitution and constitutional court, the American board regime has tended to undermine the faculty's right to participate. This was the topic of a conference of the American Association of University Professors with the title "Shared Governance vs. Corporate Management" in 1996. One speaker whose report was entitled "The Strange Death of Faculty Governance?" concluded: "A wide variety of campuses, from private to public, are experiencing the gradual displacement of regular faculty governance in favor of hierarchical corporate decision-making structures." [27]

---

[27] Joanna Vecchiarelli Scott, "The Strange Death of Faculty Governance?" *Political Science and Politics* 29.4 (1996): 724.

b) The financial support for the system of higher education is a consequence of "societal value judgments that set certain priorities within the funds which are to be allocated." [28] This statement of Daxner's applies first and foremost for Germany, where the system of public support for all facilities of the tertiary education sector dominates. In the USA, the state institutions of higher learning are supported up to 50 % by the federal and individual state and local governments; the private institutions receive predominantly federal funds (14 %). Here the proportion of fees (43%) and endowments (5 %) supporting the institution is higher than at the state institutions of higher learning (approximately 18 % and 3 %). The income from university services and commercial ventures is considerable (each approximately 23 %). In addition, there are endowments, donations, etc. (8.3 % and 5.7 %). Fundraising, which means the acquisition of public and private funds, takes place in the form of a dynamic competion for money – in contrast to the German system of a long-term allocation of personnel and materials fixed in the state budget by law.

American business has a different relationship to institutions of higher learning in as far as it becomes financially engaged not only in business related fields but also for liberal arts and social science research objectives in the form of allocating endowment capital and donations. It is often obviously guided by self-serving interests and promoted by corresponding tax laws governing charitable giving. The loyalty of the alumni for their institution of higher education contributes to this. At any rate, approximately 8 % of an institution of higher education's income stems from this source. German business has to date developed no such relationship to institutions of higher learning, which they regard to be the business of the state to be carried on according to their expectations. Private funding is either short-term, like the cash injections for chairs, or of relatively limited scope in the case of donations. This reciprocal lack of familiarity between businesses and universities reveals itself in two German phenomena:

ba) With the exception of the Witten/Herdecke University and special business oriented institutions of higher learning, private institutions supported by fees and business funding have not arisen. [29] The reason behind this is that, as a rule, all levels of society are in the final analysis convinced of the rightness of governmental monopoly over higher education.

bb) For the first time, government initiatives are attempting to set up an

---

[28] Daxner 185.

[29] Cf. Konrad Schily, "Witten/Herdecke – Still (?) A Special Case Among Universities in Germany," in this volume.

American-style cooperation between university research and its commercialization by private business in Germany.

4. Concluding comment

A system of higher education is not only an integral component of a societal order, but also an expression of its modernity, which in turn is dependent upon the development of the "productive force" of scholarship. It is for this reason that the investments in education and research on the part of government and business are decisive in the long term in society's material well-being and cultural quality of life. As long as the German reform discourse about the future of the educational system is not linked to the question of whether society is prepared to make such investments, it will always be a slave to empty coffers. The reduction in educational expenditures in the past few years to 5.1 % of the GNP is not insignificant in comparison to the US (7.1 %). In the last analysis, one should not regard the societal value decision in favor of increased spending for education and research exclusively from the standpoint of the utilitarian logic of economic prosperity. For however a modern system of higher education should look, the measure against which its achievement is judged remains the substantive rationality of "scholarship as a way of life"; this is the source of the life of reason in society.

This set of objectives for a reformed university should also provide the decisive criterion for the selective appropriation of certain components of the American system of higher education. American experts unanimously agree that a total transfer of the system is out of the question, to which a German observer can only agree. After all the American system is also the subject of crisis talk which began years ago with Allan Bloom's polemic. [30] And yet an intelligent and concept-conscious reflection of the American experience should provide the German reform discourse with important impulses for the restructuring of the German higher educational landscape, which is required for the sake of its future.

---

[30]   Allan Bloom, *The Closing of the American Mind*, (New York: Simon and Schuster, 1987); on the more recent discussion: Christopher Lucas, *Crisis in the Academy*, (New York: St. Martin's, 1995); Bill Readings, *The University in Ruins* (Cambridge, Mass. : Harvard UP, 1995); Louis Menand, ed., *The Future of Academic Freedom* (Chicago: Chicago UP, 1995).

OBSERVATIONS ON AMERICAN HIGHER EDUCATION: IS THE AMERICAN SYSTEM RELEVANT FOR GERMANY?

I. Michael HEYMAN

The papers in this volume are devoted to a comparison of higher education in Germany and the United States and to a discussion of how the two systems cope with contemporary pressures and seek to take advantage of opportunities. My remarks are not intended to provide answers to the issues that will be addressed. Rather, they are to set the stage by observations and questions which others will discuss in detail. [1]

It is useful at the outset to define the particular subjects we will be engaging. They represent interrelated problems of the moment. There are many: Governance; Costs and Funding; Differentiation; Teaching and Research; Status of Faculty (Tenure and Irregulars); Liberal Arts and Career Preparation (Measuring Outcomes and Defining Missions); Diversity of Participants; Quality, Nature, and Funding of Research.

Most of these issues are grounded in the enlargement of access and the concomitant huge increase in student numbers in the last forty years or so. The

---

I. Michael HEYMAN: Former Secretary of the Smithsonian Institution (until 1999), former Counselor to the Secretary and Deputy Assistant Secretary for Policy at the Department of the Interior, and former Chancellor and Professor Emeritus at the University of California, Berkeley; he has served on and chaired numerous boards and commissions and has written numerous articles, papers, and legal documents in the area of civil rights, constitutional law, land planning, metropolitan government, housing, environmental law and management, public land law and affirmative action.

[1] The conference documented here was not the first, nor will it have been the last. Societal demands and the dynamic evolution of systems of higher education change frames of reference and require further analysis and discussion. Prior conferences have been enlightening and papers emanating from them instructive. I am especially grateful to the reports from the conference "German and American Universities: Mutual Influences in Past and Present" held in May 1991 at the City University of New York. Its papers were published as *German and American Universities: Mutual Influences – Past and Present*, eds. Ulrich Teichler and Henry Wasser (Kassel: Wiss. Zentrum für Berufs- und Hochschulforschung, 1992). The papers by Claudius Gellert and Henry Wasser have been most helpful for me.

reasons for growth are numerous. The major ones are related to demography, political change, and the demands of our economies. Student numbers might not rise as rapidly in the future, but they surely will not diminish.

The questions we face are how to cope with this growth while assuring, to the extent feasible, a number of outcomes. Among these are:

– Meaningful educational experiences for students with differing attainments and aspirations;
– Fulfilling and energizing careers for faculty;
– An inclusionary predisposition, both to afford equality of opportunity and, eventually, to minimize discord;
– Excellent intellectual product in scholarship and research;
– Reasonable efficiency in accomplishing the goals; and
– A sensible and acceptable distribution of costs.

We in Germany and America deal with similar problems, but in different cultural milieu. Many of us have done work in comparative fields – in social sciences, humanities, and the professions. Mine, in a university context, has been mainly in law, urban planning, and conservation. I have found that comparative studies can provide exceedingly interesting insights. But I have never found that broad solutions are transferable from one culture to another. Therefore, I caution that the prospect of wholesale adoption of any particular system of organization or means towards desirable ends is illusory. For instance, later in this presentation I will talk about the tripartite systems of public higher education in California. Many insights can be learned from understanding these systems. I cannot imagine it would be profitable, however, to contemplate installation of these systems wholesale in places other than where they evolved.

Having issued this warning, it is nevertheless useful to see how today's organization of higher education in Germany and the United States has intertwined roots. Looking at origins from the American perspective, much is owed to both Germany and England.

From England came the conception of a close relationship between teachers and students concerning defined subject matter and a preoccupation with developing a cultured, educated, and worthy graduate. From Germany came a different conception, less focussed on imparting a body of knowledge by faculty to student, but based rather on the idea of a functional unity between teaching and research, with learning occurring as a by-product of collaborative research which produced new knowledge in the quest for both theory and objective truth. Thus subject, rather than the personal development of the student, received primary attention.

The structure of American universities reflects these two roots. From England comes the undergraduate curriculum with its liberal arts core and from Germany the basic methodology of graduate education in the arts and sciences with less emphasis on courses and primary reliance on both individual and collaborative research. An American contribution is the introduction of the professional school into the university mix. An interesting by-product of this has been the pervasive influence of the preoccupations and methodologies of university education in arts and sciences on the curricula of professional schools.

Most universities and colleges in the United States until the mid-19th Century featured curriculum classical in nature with little emphasis on sciences or technology. Most were private, with ultimate governance the responsibility of privately-chosen boards of trustees, and most of the institutions were religious in origin, although many had become secular in nature.

Against this background, a relatively unique American contribution of the 19th Century was the creation of land grant public institutions of higher education, which offered much broader access to students than the private counterparts, especially at the undergraduate level, a research-oriented graduate education on the German model in the humanities and social and natural sciences, and a much broader curriculum covering practical arts (engineering, for instance) as well as more conventional subjects. As so often happens in the United States, the land grant universities joined the panoply available; they did not substitute for existing institutions, but the new philosophy had fundamental impacts on higher education in general.

I indicated at the outset that the huge enlargement of access to higher education is the central factor with which systems of higher education in Germany and the United States must cope. The United States, while not without problems, has done relatively well. In a few moments, I will discuss briefly how structured diversification has developed in the United States.

Germany, according to a number of commentators, has had greater difficulty: There has been diversification of the German system of higher education by rapid expansion of an already existing post-secondary non-university sector (analogous to British poly-technics) and the upgrading of institutions from secondary to the post-secondary level. Moreover, new universities have been set up. Nevertheless, there are problems. I quote in this regard from Gellert's article previously referenced:

> In Germany the expansion of the university system after World War II has led to an awkward structural and functional muddle. The transformation of the system into places of mass higher education with about four times more students now than in the early sixties, has jeopardized the traditional balance between the

tasks of academic inquiry and advanced training of students. The old ideal of a unity of research and teaching is still part of the official value frame of reference at universities. But in recent decades frictions occurred in this system because of an increasing discrepancy between the traditional research orientation of university teachers and their actual involvement in professional or even vocational training of large numbers. Thus, despite several decades of reform discussions, this model is still characterized by antagonistic structural features: on the one hand, the students' ability to choose freely subject, universities, and their time of examination; on the other, the professors' freedom to teach whatever they like (both sanctioned by the Humboldtian principle of the freedom of teaching and learning). Other significant aspects have been the constitutionally guaranteed open access to all universities for anybody with a ... secondary degree; the bureaucratic and state control of all curricular and organizational matters, including the civil service status of the professorate; the overloading of programmes and courses according to individual research interests of the professors; and finally, the widely criticized length of studies in most subject areas. (50)

I cannot attest to the accuracy of these observations, but if they were accurate in 1991 and largely persist today, the purposes of the conference documented here are obvious.

Let me turn in somewhat greater detail to the American experience. I will use California as an example for many reasons:

1. Familiarity – I taught and administered at the University of California, Berkeley for 35 years.
2. A huge state, normally on the forefront of change. A place of diversity – leading the country in this regard. The population in 1995 was over 31.5 million. Estimated population in 2010 is a third more. On the verge of minority majority with an extensive Latino population, a growing Asian-American component and African-Americans at a steady 10 percent. Nevertheless, by referendum, the use of race as a criterion for public benefits was banned and benefits for immigrants (especially illegals) were curtailed.
3. A very large student population in higher education. Fall enrollment in 1997 was over 1.8 million. 85 percent were in public institutions. Minority enrollment was likewise hefty consisting of 47.9 percent in 1995. In 1993 – 4, California institutions awarded 121,000 bachelor degrees, 38,700 masters, and over 5000 doctorates.
4. A well articulated system of public higher education with access guaranteed to all high school graduates to two-year community colleges, but with largely merit-based admission to state colleges and to the University of California. In addition, a vigorous private sector, with both research universities (principally Stanford and the University of Southern California) and liberal

arts colleges, both secular and religious. Public institutions, however, as indicated, predominate. There are 108 community colleges, 28 state colleges and 9 (to be 10) University of California campuses.

My impressionistic sense is that this system does relatively well in assuring positive outcomes in relation to the criteria I posited at the outset.

– The diversification of institutions fairly well provides meaningful educational experiences for a wide range of students with differing attainments and aspirations. And it is a second chance system. Thus, those who perform well in community college have opportunities to transfer to both higher systems after graduation.

– Regular faculty seem well treated with ample opportunity at the state college level, and especially at the University, to do meaningful research. Problems exist, however, for non-regular faculty.

– Inclusionary efforts are, on the one hand, made more difficult by segmentation. On the other hand, all are assured a place somewhere with upward transfer possible. The recent referendum rejecting affirmative action, however, has a decidedly negative impact, especially at the most sought-after campuses of the University. Tendencies towards de facto segregation by campus are maximized.

– Concentrating much of the serious research effort at university campuses assures excellent intellectual product. Teaching loads are not substantial impediments, especially in the physical and natural sciences. New patterns of funding of research raise some serious problems. Segmentation, in most ways, helps efficient outcomes.

– Much heavier reliance on tuition than was previously true impacts access and raises serious equity problems which are somewhat ameliorated by student aid.

Many of these aspects will be addressed in the other papers of this volume.

Finally, I turn to more generally-perceived problems in American higher education. I was privileged to serve on a Commission of the Association of Governing Boards of Universities and Colleges in 1996 which concluded that serious governance problems affect many institutions of higher education in the United States, especially in the public sector. The report called for a strengthened role for academic presidents. The conclusion has been hotly debated, especially in faculty circles, but there is greater agreement concerning the nature of the problems sought to be addressed.

I will address three clusters of problems: diminishing resources, impacts of information technology, and access and diversity of student body and faculty.

I leave governance to the next two papers. Before I do this, let me stress again the enormous variation of educational institutions in the United States: public and private; military and civilian; church run, church affiliated, and staunchly non-religious; technical institutes; liberal arts colleges; two-year community colleges; small and comprehensive universities; corporation run training and education programs. I stress this because the problems being faced by higher education in general have variable impacts depending upon type of institution.

First, diminishing resources. The United States economy is now very robust with surpluses occurring in federal and state coffers and large aggregations of capital in the hands of a large number (although a small percentage) of Americans. It was not long ago, however, that public-sector resources were less, and public spending for higher education waned, establishing new patterns which will likely persist with public expenditures in the educational sector focussed on K-12.

This means: (1) that public resources for general support for higher education will not be copious (including student financial aid so important to the private sector), and (2) the higher levels of tuition that have occurred in the last decade in the public sector, and longer in the private, will persist.

High tuition has galvanized public scrutiny resulting in questioning, for instance, of:

1. Personnel practices, most notably tenure, and the use of graduate students and adjunct faculty to teach undergraduate courses;
2. The relevancy of liberal arts curricula to career aspirations;
3. Enrollment limits on core courses in large universities, extending time to degree;
4. And the "failure" to incorporate efficiencies of the business world – for instance, downsizing – by the more extensive use of information technology.

Higher education is seeking to respond to the bleaker resource picture (and the criticism that has ensued), but the responses raise other problems. For instance, private fund raising efforts have intensified, but concomitantly so has the proportion of time devoted to these efforts by administrators and faculty, thus lessening attention to the teaching and research programs. Additionally, corporate support is playing a larger role, especially in research, which raises dangers to free flow of information and to the nature of research being undertaken. Another example is the increasing use of irregular faculty (not on tenure tracks, being paid less and teaching more, unrewarded for research, often without fringe benefits) in order to reduce costs and maintain greater flexibility to respond to accelerating change.

Second, information technology: The higher education sector (other than scientific research) is embracing information technology more slowly than many other sectors, but incorporation is inevitable. There are obvious applications in management information and administration, and they are being used, as are means of individual communication like E-mail. Less rapid, however, is inclusion in various ways in courses, although such use is accelerating as younger faculty become proportionally more numerous and student expectations increase. The use of information technology techniques to substitute for more conventional forms of instruction, however, seems to be moving quite slowly.

On the horizon, however, is a whole new means for delivering instruction. Concepts like virtual university, distance learning, and the like, are becoming current. The impacts of these developments are uncertain. But their prospects are troubling for residentially-oriented undergraduate experiences and collaborative forms of graduate education. They clearly provide significant potential, in any event, for post-university education.

By way of conclusion I want to turn very briefly to access and the diversity of student bodies and faculty. America, in my view, is at a fascinating point in history, as its population becomes less reflective of Caucasians of European origin. This change is leading, as we should expect, to others (minorities in the current vocabulary) occupying higher proportions of the collective student body than heretofore. But the distribution among institutions is far from even with minorities disproportionately located in the less prestigious part of the higher education spectrum. Race-sensitive criteria, as part of affirmative action, were helping to address this disproportionality, but its rejection is a backward step, in my view, to producing an integrated leadership in the near future in important sectors like government and business.

Governance and Funding of Universities in the United States: The Example of Ohio

Alan Geiger

In the United States, in many ways, education is fraught with politics. I suspect the same is true in Germany. How then, do these political interests interact for us in the state of Ohio and are we different from the other 49 states? The picture I will paint here will probably seem unclear, maybe unfocused – but it is true.

I will begin by outlining the various elements of higher education in our states, their roles and something about the players. These include and begin with the federal government and extend to national or regional accreditation agencies, state government, state controlling or coordinating boards, boards of trustees and in some cases some form of local or community interests.

My responsibility entails dealing with these entities. I want to focus on those areas I most personally interact with, i.e., state government, state boards and boards of trustees. These sectors are where the greatest differences exist between the two educational systems represented here. But before I begin that discussion I want to address two other contributing aspects to this matter one should know about.

First is that of the university presidency. Let me broadly describe the presidency, as I know it, and then discuss how, in the case of Ohio University, the president engages the aforementioned elements of our higher education system. And, secondly, I will cover my role and responsibilities as assistant to the president, secretary to the board of trustees, and legislative liaison.

Alan Geiger: Assistant to the President, Secretary of the Board of Trustees, Director of Governmental Relations at Ohio University; his other positions and responsibilities include membership in the Athens County Economic Development Council, Vice President of the Athens Area Chamber of Commerce, former University Facilities Planner and Director of Construction, and former Assistant Director at Ohio University Innovation Center.

THE PRESIDENCY

When one considers governance and legal matters in our higher education system the focus is often on the president. Some would say the successful president has as key advisors an attorney, a lobbyist and a media relations person – all responsible for keeping him or her out of "trouble." In presenting the roles of our board of trustees later, one will note its most critical role is the appointment or dismissal of the president. Likewise, the president knows and understands that the presidential appointment is at the discretion of the board of trustees. From a corporate sense, the president's decisions become our university's "laws" and may trigger other legal issues. This results in a myriad of policies and procedures by which we operate. These vary from how appointments are made to how sick leave and vacation time may be taken, to matters of business data processing, administration, development and planning, and student issues.

The notion of student matters deserves more attention. We have what I call a quasi-legal system in place, called the Student Code of Conduct, under which two levels of offenses may be charged. The judicial process adjudicates about 2,000 cases a year. Most are of a minor nature, including property damage, alcohol and other similar type abuse, primarily a student-against-student issue. A handful of more serious offenses do occur annually and these trouble us deeply. Sanctions vary, depending upon the offense and findings, and in the most serious of cases, appeals are permitted directly to the president. Our university system is independent of civil or criminal proceedings. They or we may take action first depending on the nature of the offense. It goes without saying there is some controversy in this type of system. However, most U.S. universities have similar ones in place. My opinion is that we will probably see, over time, modifications to this system bringing it more in line with our laws and courts.

The president, acting within his capacity to see that the institution is well-managed and within the scope of his responsibilities, is normally indemnified for university-resultant suits and ultimately individually dismissed. The same holds true for our trustees. The myriad of legal issues the President deals with run the gamut and consume a significant portion of his time. Involved are federal courts to local common pleas court, Ohio Court of Claims, unemployment compensation claims, collection suits, environmental claims, suits involving our medical center, complaints to the Inspector General and Ethics Commission, discrimination claims, labor matters, patents and licensing, trademarks and logo licensing, federal communication matters and real estate issues. This list is long, but the good news is that there are limited numbers of cases associated with each area and our potential financial exposure is about $6 million (U.S.), much of which will be funded from outside our university sources.

The nature of our legal suits include: a student suing us for expulsion citing denial of constitutional rights, sex discrimination cases, malpractice cases against our medical residents and physicians, complaints filed by faculty alleging a violation of ethics laws or discrimination, salary issues, labor matters involving workers' compensation claims, arbitration, discipline, removal and classification matters, contesting with a younger school to our north about the use of our name "Ohio" and purchasing and leasing of real estate.

THE ASSISTANT TO THE PRESIDENT, ET. AL.

My role and responsibilities as Assistant to the President, Secretary to the Board of Trustees and Legislative Liaison are somewhat unique to our higher education administrative structure. Unique in terms of responsibilities held, perhaps; but those responsibilities are collectively important because they reinforce and affirm our key relationships with others.

Let's begin in the simplest fashion. The assistant to the president is not the second in command of the university. Rather, I do what the president says or doesn't want to do. As Secretary to the Board of Trustees I help guide the trustees and serve as a go-between for the trustees and president. With my legislative hat on, I attempt to anticipate statewide issues and keep the president out front of them with no surprises.

As it relates to our subject matter, this combination of roles does several things. First, it provides almost instant credibility since the assumption is made that I probably know what the president and trustees are thinking. Second, it creates in others, a sense of trust and confidence in me personally since the institution's faith is placed in me. And third, it signals to others, maybe even to competitors, that I have the strength of the institution behind me. Finally, all this marshals alumni of your institution who are somehow involved with state government to support both me and their institution.

FEDERAL GOVERNMENT AND LOCAL INTERESTS

I am very much aware that we do not live and function in isolation, particularly in relationship to government and legal issues. These entities help frame what we do and I want to identify these for my purposes.

While not a direct responsibility of the federal government, higher education is impacted by the Feds on several fronts, all of which are important to us.

For example, most student financial aid programs evolve at the federal level and they are the major sources of financial aid for our students. Most recently the federal government has initiated new programs to provide some income tax relief under certain circumstances, from college and university costs. Federally sponsored and contract research support is important to most all institutions of higher education. In Ohio University's case, such federal support is in the neighborhood of $35 million annually which is about 10% of our annual total budget. The federal government and its agencies affect us as well by affirmative action initiatives, minimum wage requirements, requirements for the care of research animals and cost of postage just to mention a few.

On the other end of the broad government continuum is local government. The small community in which the Ohio University is located is called Athens and is in fact a namesake of the Greek City of Athens. We are a town of slightly over 26,000 whose population – independent of the students, faculty and staff – is less than 6,000 persons. We are a company town whose business is education. We are the economic base of the community and region and are often criticized by the citizenry and local government as being heavy-handed and insensitive to business and other issues or concerns. All this comes with the territory.

The government and legal issues for us and our city officials are quite different than those at the macro federal level. And by the way, we are exempted by state law from local codes and ordinance. Here our concerns deal with more mundane matters, such as does the water flow in and the sewage out; if needed, can fire protection be provided; and are other services being provided that ensure for the well-being of all inhabitants of our fair city. Whether dealing with federal or local government, politics prevail.

ACCREDITATION AGENCIES

Opportunity also involves another such entity, the North Central Association of Colleges and Schools, Commission on Institution of Higher Education. In 1993, this association visited, reviewed a self-study and granted (renewed) Ohio University's status as mature, doctoral-granting institution, district-wide to include its regional campus. Such an accreditation, in this case every ten years, looks at a host of factors such as initiating governance, planning, financial resources, internal and external review and accreditation, assessment of student satisfactions and outcomes, degree granting units, and so on.

In addition to this university-wide type accreditation there are numerous others – evaluating departments, colleges and so on. The broad purposes of such efforts in North Central Ohio Association is to:

1. Develop accreditation processes which encourages quality and educational excellence.
2. Stimulate improvement of educational programs and effectiveness of instruction, with concern for freedom to teach and learn.
3. Establish criteria which, when met, entitle educational institutions to receive the status of accreditation, and to establish procedures by which the determination of accreditation is made.
4. Establish criteria which, when met, entitle educational institutions to be affiliated with the association in ways other than membership, and to establish procedures by which the determination of such affiliation is made.

STATE GOVERNMENT

Higher education in the United States is seen, for the most part, as the responsibility of individual states and in turn, is a product of history, political whim and the cultures of each of the 50 states. In our state of Ohio, government's role is to provide broad oversight, financial support, laws and regulations to function by and in some rare cases, even to deal with individual quirks of legislative members. The General Assembly, our House and Senate, hold our well being in their hands, and though we try to shake their hands, we also lobby them to do right by us.

For reference, Ohio's State Government contains three branches: executive, legislative, and judicial. The State's web page describes them thusly:

The *Executive branch* includes the Governor, Lieutenant Governor, Secretary of State, Auditor of State, Attorney General, Treasurer of State, State Board of Education and the Governor's Cabinet. The Cabinet members serve as directors for the many state agencies and are appointed by the Governor. The executive branch is overall responsible for the setting of higher education policy in the state.

Unfortunately, and in Ohio's case, there is no cabinet-level position for higher education and, therefore, depending on the issue, we may or may not find the support sought. I am going to discuss the Ohio Board of Regents later, but you will see it is only a recommending/coordinating board. Thus, persuasion becomes the vehicle for influence. It does not hurt our interests that the recent two-term governor is a graduate of our university or that many key administrative officers are graduates and may in fact have children in attendance. On the other hand I do sometimes wonder if this connection does not limit their support for fear of being partisan. The important factor here is that we do have ready access to these leaders and I believe, some influence, in matters important to us.

The Legislative branch consists of the House of Representatives and the Senate. Together, these bodies are referred to as "The General Assembly." Ohio's House of Representatives has 99 members; the Senate has 33. *The Legislative Service Commission*, a staff of trained legal experts and personnel, drafts proposals for new laws and law changes, and is one of several *legislative agencies* that are also part of the Legislative branch of Ohio's state government.

The legislative branch is where most of the political action occurs and it's there that our fate is decided. As with the executive branch, we are fortunate to have established relationships with individual members and their collective leadership. Several have or have had their sons and daughters at our university. We also have long-standing support from key staffers, many of whom form the "Ohio University Mafia." This group of 120 or so individuals keeps the president and me informed – before many of our colleagues – of critical issues, their timing and chances for success. Without this type of support the university would probably need a full-time lobbying effort in Columbus as opposed to me being there parttime. You cannot have too many good friends.

The *Judicial branch* comprises the Ohio Supreme Court; numerous judiciary bodies – including 12 courts of appeals, courts of common pleas in each county, municipal courts, and many county courts; and the Court of Claims.

When we find ourselves before a branch of the judiciary we are usually disadvantaged, or seen as the big bully. State universities are limited in how they can legally defend or represent themselves. Much of the disadvantage comes from the political nature of counsel assignments and the sympathy of some courts or judges to the perceived so-called private underdog. While we enjoy some legal authority, because we are part of state government, the university uses this authority carefully and conservatively. As one might suspect, we have many, many more suits against as opposed to those we file.

There are two matters to note here as state government impacts our university. The first is term limits for state elected officials. A limit of eight consecutive years of House or Senate service went into effect in 1992. Thus, our long-time friends will be mostly gone by the year 2000. To me, this is the real Y-2K problem! Higher education's agenda takes time to develop and to build a sense of trust and confidence with political leaders. With term limits, the traditional style of leadership is gone. Members now have their own agenda, and little time to accomplish it. The fallout from this is not all negative in that the status of individuals like me may be one of more influence than we might have enjoyed in the past.

The second matter is support for higher education in the state budget. Ohio's budget is about $36 billion biannually. Over the past decade higher education's share has dropped from over 13% to 11%. We also find ourselves below the priorities of health and welfare, prisons, and elementary and secondary education. Elementary and secondary education has sued the state seeking more funding, alleging an unequal funding formula within this system, and should this suit be successful, more funding from an already strong state economy will go there. Our biggest fears with state budget matters are the loss of priority and the possibility that more and more state funding will be earmarked elsewhere – all to the detriment of higher education. We are becoming a state where the discretionary portion of the state's budget is shrinking. This does not bode well for us.

STATE OVERSIGHT BOARDS

The major oversight board in our state is the Ohio Board of Regents. This board is a recommending and coordinating board, as opposed to other U.S. State systems where more control and authority rest at the central level. We are fortunate at Ohio University to enjoy so much university autonomy.

The Regents' web page describes them thusly:

The Ohio Board of Regents is an eleven-member public body created by the state in 1963 to:
1. Provide higher education policy advice to the Governor and General Assembly
2. Map strategies involving the state's colleges and universities
3. Advocate for and manage distribution of state support for public colleges and universities
4. Implement statewide legislative mandates.

The Governor appoints the nine voting members of the Board who serve 9-year terms. The chairs of the General Assembly's Education Committees serve as non-voting ex-officio members of the Board. The Regents appoint a Chancellor to serve as their chief administrative officer. At the moment two former Ohio University trustees sit as Regents; something we had a little to do with, but by and large, these appointments traditionally are political ones or ones favoring contributors.

For the record, Ohio's system of higher education is composed of more than 100 colleges and universities, including 38 separately governed state-assisted colleges and universities.

In the fall of 1998, Ohio's public colleges and universities enrolled 411,446 students. Independent (private) colleges and universities enrolled 114,476 students.

Our individual and institutional relationships with the Regents are tops in the state and we serve as a sounding board for many of their initiatives. Examples of such interaction include the President serving on the state funding commission, participation in early review of revised funding formulas and proposed policies, testifying to promotional support for state issues, and working closely with their legislative staff, to name a few.

UNIVERSITY BOARD OF TRUSTEES

With regard to university governance, the greatest difference between our United States systems, both public and private institutions, is the concept of trusteeship. Our trustees, a body of 9 – with two non-voting student trustees – is the politic body for Ohio University. These individuals, with the exception of two-year student terms, are appointed to nine-year terms by the governor and confirmed by the State Senate. John W. Nason, in his book *The Nature of Trusteeship* describes 13 responsibilities of individual trustees and their boards.

1. To maintain the integrity of the Trust.
2. To appoint the President.
3. To make certain that the institution is well managed.
4. To approve the budget
5. To raise money.
6. To manage the Endowment.
7. To assure adequate physical facilities.
8. To oversee the Educational Program.
9. To approve long range plans.
10. To serve as bridge and buffer between campus and community.
11. To preserve institutional autonomy.
12. To serve as court of appeal.
13. To be informed.

For me, this list is both practical and comprehensive. This is simply another way of describing stewardship. Trustees' roles and responsibilities are further defined by the Ohio Revised Code. In a nutshell, they may do all things necessary for the creation, proper maintenance, and continuous and successful operation of the institution. Examples of specific stewardship at Ohio University are defined by three broad policy areas: The lists by areas are long, but reciting them gives one an appreciation for the scope of trusteeship.

The first area involves matters of budget, finance and facilities. Stewardship here includes:

a) the University's budgets, schedule of student fees, financial operations, business organization and practices, borrowing of funds, investment of funds, and submission of appropriation requests;

b) solicitation of funds, relations with local, state and federal legislative and administrative agencies, and promotion of alumni activities;

c) naming, location, planning, construction, and maintenance of the University's plant and grounds, and the purchase and sale of lands and building.

The second area is one of educational policies and includes:

a) research policies and activities;

b) academic appointment, promotion, and tenure policies and procedures;

c) areas of instruction;

d) awarding of degrees;

e) student financial aids;

f) intercollegiate athletics;

g) student life and student services;

h) student admissions and enrollment.

The third and final area deals with executive level matters and includes:

a) salary, wage, and benefit policies;

b) appointment of senior administrative officers;

c) general university policies and business.

In essence, the task of the assistant to the president has been described according to Reinhold Niebuhr's well-known dictum: to ask for courage to know the things that can and cannot be changed and the wisdom to know the difference.

CHANGING PATTERNS OF GOVERNANCE AND FINANCE IN GERMAN HIGHER EDUCATION

Hans N. WEILER

I

This paper is about Germany, but it is not only about Germany. It is about the funding of higher education, but it is not only about funding.

I am drawing most of my evidence from German higher education, but I am also reaching out into the experience of other Western countries (mainly the ones belonging to the OECD), including from time to time the United States, in order to highlight both underlying commonalities and important differences in higher education policy.

I am primarily interested in questions of funding in higher education, but I have learned that there is no way to treat questions of funding as separate from questions of governance and decision-making. I am therefore treating the issue of funding as a key element in the governance of higher education. I will argue, in fact, that the issue of funding can serve as a lens through which the entire issue of structural reform in higher education can be most clearly observed.

In addition to the documentary evidence, I have drawn on my own experience both as a faculty member and administrator at a major private university in the United States – Stanford University – where I worked for nearly thirty years, and as the head of a new institution of higher education – Viadrina European University – which was founded in the Eastern part of Germany in 1991. Both institutions, albeit in very and instructively different ways, have faced

Hans N. WEILER: Professor of Education and Political Science, Emeritus, Stanford University; former *Rektor* (president) of the Europa-Universität Viadrina at Frankfurt (Oder) (until 1999); former Director of UNESCO's International Institute for Educational Planning, Paris; advisory appointments with the World Bank, the Ford Foundation, the state government of Saxony and other national and international agencies. Current interests include the comparative politics of reform in higher education, the relationship between university finance and university governance, and the politics of knowledge production.

and continue to face some of the very issues in financing that have occupied the broader OECD discussion over the past decade. [1]

As one of the most prestigious and selective private institutions of higher learning in the United States, Stanford has over the last two decades witnessed the blurring of the distinctions between public and private higher education in the US, has faced growing governmental pressure for accountability especially in its sponsored research programs, has played a major role in moderating the market forces in higher education through programs of need-blind admissions and affirmative action, and continues to face the increasingly difficult task of reconciling rising cost and limitations to price increases in its tuition and indirect cost rates.

My experience of planning and building for the past seven years a new university in Germany is of a rather different, but I think similarly instructive kind. As a university built literally and deliberately on the border between Germany and Poland, committed to making a significant contribution to the renewal and strengthening of the relationship between these two countries, and located in one of the more economically deprived areas of what used to be the German Democratic Republic, Viadrina European University has a good deal in common with both its fellow universities in the rest of Germany – East and West – and some of the newly developing universities in Central and Eastern Europe. With regard to the issue of higher education financing and governance, the Viadrina is right now in a state of transition from less autonomy from the state to more autonomy, from line-item systems of budgeting to more lump-sum and "global" patterns of resource allocation, and from fairly automated systems of internal resource distribution to much more performance-based systems in allocating resources both to individual institutions and within institutions to individual operating units. In addition, there is by now in Germany a debate of unprecedented intensity on both the question of tuition (which thus far does not exist, and which I happen to think should exist) and on the further growth of the (as yet insignificant) private sector in German higher education. Since I have become an active participant in these debates (recently, among other things, as chair of a panel set up to assess a number of projects for new private institutions in higher education), I have developed some first-hand knowledge not only of the issues, but also of the extraordinary level of political conflict that can develop around them.

---

[1]   Organisation for Economic Co-operation and Development (OECD), *Financing Higher Education: Current Patterns* (Paris: OECD, 1990).

II

My second preliminary remark has to do with the relationship between higher education and championship soccer. I know, after all, what I owe a city like Munich. I do not want to overdo the analogy between the financing of higher education and the playing of championship soccer, but I couldn't help but being struck by some obvious similarities and even by some lessons one might learn about higher education on the soccer field.

Some parallels are pretty obvious. In higher education as in soccer, one needs a lot of support, financial as well as psychological. In both, sponsors are becoming almost as important as players. Also, both higher education and soccer have a strong competitive element – even though there are always some universities and some soccer teams that behave as if competition did not exist; they both risk defeat. And again in both soccer and higher education, you need some kind of an outside referee to keep you honest, to tell you when you have gone too far in one direction so that you have to be called offsides, and to show you a red card when you have violated the rules of the game. German higher education (to its detriment, I believe) tends to rely on a single referee – the state, whose conception of the game is very limited indeed.

But the two lessons that I find most instructive for higher education as I watch the drama of championship soccer unfold are of a different kind: The first lesson has to do with the role of money. God knows money is important in soccer, and god knows just as well that money is important in higher education. But when you look a little more closely, it becomes very clear that money isn't everything, and that in higher education as in soccer, success is as much a result of financial conditions as it is of good and convincing ideas, of creativity and inspiration, of perseverance and determination. As head of a young and struggling university, I am the last one to think little of the question of funding, but I also know that, without a lot of good ideas, even a lot of money will not get you very far in higher education.

The other lesson has to do with how successful teams operate. Look at a winning team, and the one thing that will strike you is how all parts work together perfectly, and how in building a winning team you cannot just concentrate on defense, or penalty kicks, or passing, or on getting the goalkeeper in top shape. The same thing goes for successful strategies in higher education: all factors need to work together, and need to be seen and understood together. My point here is that one cannot look at financing in isolation from all other aspects of higher education. There is a close and very important relationship between the financial arrangements in higher education, on the one hand, and the administrative relationship between the state and universities, or the internal organizational characteristics of universities, or the process of setting academic goals in teaching and research, on the other. Understanding the financing of education means understanding these complex relationships, and it is to some of these that I now turn.

III

I propose to organize my review of recent trends and developments in the governance and financing of higher education around a number of key issues that proceed somewhat loosely from a macro to a micro level, and will at the end, in a final section, raise a few broader themes in higher education policy that I regard as worth keeping in mind as one debates different options in financing and governance.

The macro/micro distinction in higher education financing is, by the way, not a particularly neat one, since many developments cut across all levels of the system; take, for example, the case of formula funding or parameter-based funding, which establishes principles and procedures both for the allocation of public resources to individual institutions and for the distribution of resources within each institution. Nonetheless, it may be useful to start with the broader view and work our way to some of the specifically institutional concerns.

As I see it, the twin goals in the current debate in Germany and among other OECD countries about the financing of higher education (and about the future shape of higher education more generally) have to do with autonomy and accountability. As institutions of higher education seek (or are pushed towards – it is not always clear which) greater autonomy from state control, there is a corresponding preoccupation with questions of accountability and transparency in the ways in which more autonomous institutions deal with their resources. Where once the state, through a tightly woven net of budgetary and other regulations, controlled or preempted a substantial part of a university's internal decision-making, policies of deregulation now confront the university with the task of designing, applying and enforcing its own ground rules for the internal allocation of resources. In the process, there is a transition from a system of control that operates "ex ante", i.e., through a set of rules and regulations set up in advance, to a steering system that works largely "ex post" and is based on allocating resources on the basis of performance. In other words: the overall tendency is from a situation where the resource situation of an institution is dependent on a given set of input parameters to a situation where output parameters are becoming more and more important. Line-item budgets, where a certain amount of money is in advance earmarked for a certain institutional purpose – e.g., the purchase of computers – are a key feature of controlling an institution "ex ante" or through the specification of inputs; by contrast, providing a university with a lump sum budget and specifying the performance criteria by which it will be judged as to whether or not it has spent this budget wisely (and should therefore receive more the next time around) controls an institution "ex post" or through its outputs.

This description may sound like a nicely professional and disinterested treatment of the transfer of responsibility for financial decision-making from the state to the universities. In actual fact, however, this transfer only thinly conceals a considerable state of emergency in the funding of higher education. In Germany and in most of the other OECD countries I know, at least part of the state's motivation for making institutions of higher education more autonomous in dealing with their financial futures has been the serious shrinking of public resources available for expanding systems of higher education. In this situation, it is very tempting for governments to transfer to the universities the increasingly unpleasant (and politically onerous) task of administering scarcity. In a review of changing financial policies in higher education in several Western European countries, the German HIS research service observes, somewhat tongue in cheek, that "the radical transition from a supply-oriented allocation of resources to a competitive allocation occurs in all countries considered against the background of a severe curtailment of funds". [2]

Be that as it may, the overall and rather fundamental change in the general pattern of funding higher education has a number of specific facets, of which I consider the following eight as being both the most significant and, from the point of view of the experience of the OECD countries and my own experience, the ones most in need of a critical assessment.

1. Changing Rationales in Budgeting and Resource Allocation: From Line-Item Budgets to Block Grants

Of all the changes in higher education financing, none has probably been more consequential than the change from line-item budgets towards global allocations or block grants, for the use of which the universities are to be responsible and accountable in an ex post manner. In the overall move towards greater autonomy of institutions of higher education, this shift has probably been the

---

[2]   Klaus Schnitzer and Foad Kazemzadeh, *Formelgebundene Finanzzuweisung des Staates an die Hochschulen – Erfahrungen aus dem europäischen Ausland* (Hannover: HIS-Hochschul-Informations-System GmbH, 1995) 9.

single most important factor. Nowhere, however, has this change been accomplished in one giant and instantaneous step. Typically, this change has been, or is being, accomplished through a gradual series of consecutive steps, such as

- allowing universities to use funds from unfilled staff positions for current operating expenditures in teaching and research, or
- making possible limited transfers between line items, or
- selecting a limited number of institutions for pilot projects to try out more encompassing schemes of block grants.

Where, as in the Netherlands, the change towards lump sum or block grant allocations has gone the farthest, it has been closely tied to a system of formulae on the basis of which the overall allocation has been determined (see below).

Without going into a great deal of technical detail here, I would like to point out a number of considerations that I have found useful as one moves in the direction of block grant funding:

a) Among the few advantages of line-item funding is the fact that budget reductions on the part of the government become more easily visible and identifiable; budget cuts can be much more easily concealed in the allocation of block grants.

b) Implicitly or explicitly, block grant allocations are tied to an underlying contractual relationship between funding agency and recipient such that, in exchange for the grant, the recipient institution engages to perform a certain set of tasks in teaching and research, the satisfactory completion of which is the university's responsibility and on the basis of which it will be supported in the next budget cycle . This kind of contract has been one of the more interesting instances of negotiation between government and universities; in current discussions in a number of German states (e.g., Lower Saxony, Berlin), where the key term is *Zielvereinbarung*, universities and the state have negotiated a fairly explicit set of development targets which the universities are committed to achieve in return for (reasonably) secure multi-year funding prospects.

c) In the United States, the National Commission on Responsibilities for Financing Postsecondary Education has a few years ago spelled out a handy set of four conditions for the success of this kind of an autonomy-accountability relationship between funding agency and recipient institutions:

   i) Agree on the tasks that need to be accomplished;

ii) Ensure that the available resources are sufficient to complete the tasks successfully;

iii) Provide the enterprise (the university) with the authority it needs to be effective, and then let it do the job without interference; and

iv) Define a set of measurements to indicate how well the enterprise is doing relative to its goals, and follow up by tracking these measurements. [3]

d) This set of ground rules already highlights the critical importance of performance measures and evaluation in making the transition to more global means of funding feasible. Here again an instructive debate on the nature and the measurement of desirable outcomes in higher education has begun in Germany, from completion rates in different programs of study to research productivity, and from the employment record of graduates to the number of scholarly awards.

e) Block grant systems allow for an important facility especially for universities in a state of transition, namely, the achievement of cross-subsidies between programs, where savings in one program can be invested in the strengthening of another.

f) From the funding agency's point of view, one of the important elements in this reshaped or reshaping world of university funding could well be the retention of a central contingency pool of resources that can be used for such purposes as

- special and particularly promising research programs,
- the support of graduate students on a competitive, cross-institutional basis,
- compensating an institution for overloads in teaching,
- bridging the time to anticipated retirements of faculty, thus making the early replacement of retiring faculty possible,
- investments in special teaching facilities, such as PC pools, or
- support of provisions for underrepresented groups, such as women students or faculty.

2. Formula Funding: New Parameters in Resource Allocation

As the pre-ordained structure of line-item budgets has begun to disappear, the need arises to find a basis on which to determine the new block grants

---

[3]   William F. Massy, *Resource Allocation Reform in Higher Education* (Washington: National Association of College and University Business Officers [NACUBO], 1994) 6-7.

or lump-sum allocations that universities are to receive under more open and autonomous funding arrangements. The search for this basis has led to a variety of "formulas" which are used to compute the funds that a university is expected to need. In this development, the Netherlands and Denmark have played the role of pioneers among OECD countries, and anybody interested in the trials and errors encountered in this process should take a close look at their experience. Other countries have taken up the challenge, and my own state, the state of Brandenburg, is now experimenting with a model of formula funding of its own, as are any number of other states in Germany and countries in Europe. In reviewing these efforts, let me emphasize the following points and observations.

a) Initially and in its strictest sense, the formulae for funding higher education have focussed on input factors, i.e. on those indicators that represent the tasks universities are supposed to perform in teaching and research, and their estimated cost. By now, however, many funding formulae have a double face: they estimate input factors, but they also tend to specify performance measures that are considered to be particularly desirable outcomes of university efforts. To give an example: One of the most fundamental elements in any funding formula is the number of students. That is a straightforward input factor. By modifying or weighing this factor in such a way as to only count students within regular graduation time limits (that is, excluding those who take forever to finish their degrees), one adds an outcome or performance measure that reflects the university's ability to provide an effective teaching program.

b) One of the difficult questions in the business of designing formulae for funding is just how finely to tune them, and whether to concentrate on a few important indicators or include as many as possible. Here, the general wisdom seems to be to focus on the ones that really matter. This is easier on the input side, where one typically limits the formula to such things as
   - the number of students (possibly modified by limiting it to students within regular graduation time), as an indicator of the load and cost of teaching;
   - the number of staff (academic and service), as an indicator of the cost incurred by their work; and
   - space, as an indicator of the cost of maintenance.

The important point about these indicators, however, is that they need to be differentially weighed, depending for example on what discipline is involved, engineering and natural science subjects requiring substantially more cost in teaching and research than humanities and social sciences. It also makes sense to weigh the number of students differentially depending on whether the instructional capacity of a given institution (as determined by its staff and space) is underutilized or overutilized; the formula we are working on in Brandenburg envisages a statistical bonus for student numbers under conditions of overutilization, and a malus or discount factor in case of underutilization.

c) On the output side, the choice of a few key indicators to include in the formula becomes more difficult, especially since this also depends on what a given institution, by the nature of its institutional mission, considers particularly important: A heavily research-oriented university will value and weigh research productivity (as measured, for example, by the elaborate peer review procedures of the UFC in Britain) and the acquisition of research funding from the outside more highly, while a more teaching-oriented school will emphasize the quality of teaching and advising and the institution's success in bringing students to an early and high-quality completion of their degree. One of the important but as yet poorly developed outcome measures would clearly be both the occupational success and the satisfaction of an institution's graduates.

d) Some funding formulae – including the ones that I have been struggling with at my institution – have an important and not adequately recognized structural deficit in that they disregard the rather simple management truth that institutions have funding needs that are independent of their size and the volume of their activities. Every university, no matter how small, needs a core admissions staff, a core personnel department, certain basic maintenance services, basic library resources, etc. The importance of this baseline estimate tends to be often overlooked when the logic of linear relations between size and funding needs prevails.

e) Funding formulas – and this is perhaps their most important function in shaping systems and institutions of higher education – serve as an important communications device: Their very composition sends a powerful message as to what is and is not considered important in a system or an institution of higher education. The relative weights given to teaching, community service, foreign student enrollment, scholarly awards, student- teacher ratio or number of women faculty all represent important value decisions for the system or the institution, and should be the result of a rather serious process of reflection and discussion.

3. Scholars and Markets: The Role of Incentives

With its increasing emphasis on output or performance criteria, formula funding contains already a substantial element of incentives for contributing to the institution's mission, and of disincentives for not contributing.

a) I would like to add to this, however, by reporting on a particularly heated debate that is being conducted in Germany right now – a debate in which, not surprisingly, the experience of American higher education serves once again as a controversial benchmark. The issue is the determination of funds that should be placed at an individual faculty member's disposal for teaching and research and, furthermore and even more delicate, the determination of a professor's compensation. At present, both of these decisions are virtually unaffected by what a professor does, what kind of a load he carries, or how he performs his tasks. The financial resources for his professorship are typically settled when he is appointed, and he has a right to receive them annually as long as the budget permits, regardless of load or performance. Similarly, professorial salaries are set by civil service guidelines and increase inexorably on the basis of only one criterion: advancing age – the only exception being a special raise available to counter an offer from another university. The current debate – fuelled by a recent resolution of the German Rectors' Conference – over changing this system with regard to both the financial resources at the professor's disposal and his salary in order to make it more incentive-oriented has all the drama of a war of religion, and may end up just as bloody. It highlights both the inherent difficulty of reform in higher education and the problems of bringing a modicum of market principles to bear upon academia.

b) On a much more minor scale, I wanted to relate an instructive example of making incentives work. I helped introduce this myself in my department at Stanford where we gave faculty members an 8% share in the overhead that the university charges on externally funded projects. Thus, for every $100,000 in sponsored research funds that a professor raised, he had $8,000 at his disposal for travel, added assistants, books, or other professional expenses. The effects were considerable.

c) Lastly, let me point out an important and often overlooked incentive that is entirely non-monetary, but in my experience extraordinarily effective. I am speaking of the devolution of decision-making, including financial decision-making, to lower levels of the organization. Being involved in decisions in such a way that one's voice does make a difference serves as a powerful motivating factor in all organizations, but particularly in a highly professionalized organization such as a university.

4. The Search for New Funds: Mobilizing External Resources

The growing shortage of public funds, combined with the desire for getting away from the state as the sole source of a university's funding, has contributed to an unprecedented preoccupation in German higher education with opening up additional and alternative sources of funding. This effort takes the form of seeking support from organized philanthropy through foundations, of a growing volume of contractual research and training programs for outside clients (for the coverage of both direct and indirect costs), of the sale of services such as language teaching or the use of libraries and data networks, the mobilization of private individual and corporate donors to set up endowment funds for special projects (such as endowed chairs), programs of continuing education, and others. Having dealt with, and carefully observed, this process in both the US and Germany, I would like to offer the following observations.

a) It is important to realize that most externally obtained resources in higher education, with the exception of endowment funding, are of questionable longevity. They typically last for a number of years, and then disappear, leaving a promising program that was funded from these sources destitute or, just as badly, dependent on the institution's regular resources. Commitments by the state to pick up the support for activities that were started with external funds are, at least in my experience, notorious for being evaded (e.g., the experience of externally funded chairs, *Stiftungslehrstühle*, in Germany in comparison with endowed chairs in the US). This situation is especially serious where, as is often the case today, state funding only covers the basics of institutional cost, while everything dynamic and innovative about an institution comes out of outside funding. As such outside funding tends to disappear over time and may not be fully replaced, the institution is left with its status-quo-oriented basic framework and sees its innovative features disappear in the process.

b) A related risk has to do with the fact that external funds tend to carry hidden costs that sometimes even the more sophisticated calculation of indirect cost will miss. These hidden costs have to do with the gradual erosion of basic capabilities in libraries, equipment and physical plant. Some of these are opportunity costs for foregoing other valuable activities in favor of an outside contract. A particularly problematic policy is that of the German national science foundation, the Deutsche Forschungsgemeinschaft, which as a matter of policy makes research awards only on the condition that the recipient institution provides all of the basic outlay – space, equipment, basic staff, and adequate library facilities. In stark contrast to this philosophy, I think it is essential that external funds cover the full cost of the services they purchase and support, including both indirect costs and the cost of developing the institution's long-term capabilities, including the training of young researchers.

c) The most important and consequential problem with outside funding in higher education, however, is the risk it carries for sustaining the institution's mission and intellectual profile. Except in the rarest case, and protestations to the contrary from the involved parties notwithstanding, the seeking of outside support typically entails compromises between the institution's own priorities and the priorities of the outside funding agency. The attempt to balance market forces with the need for institutional coherence remains in most instances imperfect, and its imperfection causes the problem of a "fragmentation of faculty allegiance" [4] between promising funding opportunities and institutional loyalties that is becoming a serious problem for a growing number of institutions of higher education.

5. Making Users Pay: Tuition and Fees in Higher Education

Given the difficulties of not only obtaining outside funds, but also of dealing with their drawbacks once they are obtained, it is not surprising that the notion of charging users for the use of higher education is gaining ground. The number of countries in the OECD where some form of tuition is charged students of higher education is increasing, and the debate about introducing tuition in those countries that do not yet have fees is heating up. This is, once again, particularly true in Germany which has a long social democratic tradition of tuition-free higher education.

a) The arguments for and against fees are fairly straightforward. At a time of shrinking resources, tuition can be a significant source of new funding. Provided one makes sure that these resources do indeed remain at the university's disposal and do not serve to offset a portion of state funding so as to cure general fiscal ailments (not an easy condition to meet, I should emphasize), substantial financial benefits can accrue from collecting even (in comparison to, say, high-price US institutions) relatively modest fees. In this connection, it seems essential that students, parents and graduates

---

4   William F. Massy, *Resource Allocation in Higher Education* (Washington: National Association of College and University Business Officers [NACUBO], 1994) 32.

have a major say in decisions about how tuition money is to be spent by the university.

b) Perhaps even more important in thinking about tuition fees is the prospect of creating more of a supply and demand dynamic in higher education. There is absolutely no question that in systems where there are fees, both universities and students behave differently. Universities tend to be more responsive to the interests and needs of fee-paying students who make a significant contribution to the financial well-being of the institution and who also have the option of taking their tuition money elsewhere. By the same token, students and their families tend to pay a good deal more attention (including critical attention) to a university education which costs them real money.

c) The main argument against tuition has been that it discriminates against students coming from economically disadvantaged groups, and that it tends to discourage those students from higher education altogether. There is some evidence from the United States that this is to some degree true, but there is also considerable evidence that this effect can be significantly moderated by appropriate programs of financial aid in connection with need-blind admission and affirmative action policies.

d) Those who argue against introducing tuition into higher education on social grounds also have to confront the argument, however, that there is nothing terribly social about a situation in which non-students who are working subsidize through their taxes the cost of university education for an upwardly mobile population of students who, by all accounts, tend to be rewarded quite generously for their degrees by significantly higher status and lifetime earnings.

e) In the end, the question of whether or not tuition in higher education can be justified hinges on the adequacy of the system of financial aid and its ability to compensate the effects of market-based tuition rates for students from disadvantaged groups. In this context, there is still much to be said for the original version of the Australian Higher Education Credit Scheme (HECS) – not the somewhat denatured version that has replaced it in the meantime – where needy students would pay both their fees and their living expenses out of a loan that is to be repaid through the tax system only if and when their later income exceeded a specified minimum income. A somewhat modified (and improved) version of this scheme has recently been proposed in Germany as well).[5]

---

[5] Stifterverband für die Deutsche Wissenschaft and Centrum für Hochschulentwicklung, *In-*

6. Private Initiatives in Higher Education: Panacea or Dead End Road?

All over the world, with the (perhaps overly) enthusiastic leadership of the World Bank, the notion of privatizing higher education has in recent years picked up a momentum of its own. Having spent most of my academic life at a private university, I am following this development with both sympathy and some concern. There is indeed much to be said for challenging the monopoly of public forms of higher education in the many countries (including Germany) where such a monopoly effectively exists, but some critical remarks are in order to keep things in perspective and to make sure that an essentially good idea does not get defeated by its own exaggerated claims.

a) In most countries of the world, including the United States though possibly excluding Brunei, higher education institutions that are entirely or even predominantly funded from private sources are simply not feasible. Even the United States that has arguably the most developed and successful system of private higher education has long moved to a hybrid situation where private institutions cover an ever increasing share of their costs from public funds – just as public universities draw increasingly on private sources of funding. Stanford and UC Berkeley provide an instructive pair in this regard.

b) What may well give the privatization of higher education a bad name is the emergence of two rather peculiar types of institutions. First, there are institutions like the ones that have recently emerged in Germany and other Western European countries that pick for themselves one or two subjects that are particularly marketable among both prospective students and corporate sponsors (usually business management and computer science), then proceed to obtain substantial resources from both corporate sponsorship and tuition fees and, in addition, seek and receive significant state subsidies. If the (excellent) idea of more privatization in higher education is to create more competition between different types of institutions, then there is no way for a fair competition to be held between these institutions and public institutions that can neither charge tuition nor market their much broader instructional spectrum, while having to maintain the full range of academic subjects over and above business and computer science. For competition to be meaningful, a level playing field is a prerequisite.

c) The other kind of newcomers in the animal kingdom of higher education are for-profit universities, of which one, the University of Phoenix, was very ably and instructively portrayed in an issue of *The New Yorker* some time

vestiF und GefoS – Modelle der individuellen und institutionellen Bildungsfinanzierung im Hochschulbereich (Gütersloh and Essen: CHE and Stifterverband, 1999).

ago.[6] I am not necessarily saying that there shouldn't be any institutions of higher education that are conducted for profit. What I am saying is that these institutions are unlikely to serve as the kind of catalyst that could help regenerate and mobilize our existing systems of public higher education.

d) Against the background of these somewhat problematic developments, we are likely to be more successful if we understand privatization not necessarily as an alternative way of funding higher education, but as an organizational and structural alternative. To introduce, even under public or partly public funding arrangements, entrepreneurial or other private management structures into higher education strikes me as an extremely worthwhile project. There are already enough examples within the overall framework of public higher education systems of running research institutes, language labs, or continuing education programs on a modified corporate model to demonstrate how much more flexibility, adaptability and innovation can thus be achieved.

7. Shaping the Institution's Profile: Steering and Controlling in Higher Education

Financing in higher education, as I have said before, is not just about money and accounting. It has a great deal to do with institutional purposes and with how they can be achieved. I happen to think that the sharpening, the cultivation of institutional purposes, the development of more specific and recognizable institutional profiles is one of the major challenges that lies ahead in German higher education. The time of the all-purpose, across-the-board university, where one could find everything but had a hard time finding excellence, is probably coming to an end. Institutions of higher education in Germany in the future will probably have a more limited, more carefully composed set of specialties, and will seek to excel in those. For this strategy to work, financing will have to play an absolutely critical part, especially in a system of allocating resources in which performance is a key determinant for funding decisions. Because if shaping and sustaining the institution's special profile is an important priority, then part of the funding formula needs to be not only the general quality of a unit's work (a department, an institute, a professor), but also the contribution which that unit makes to enhancing the university's special profile.

---

[6] James Traub, "Drive Thru U.: Higher Education for People Who Mean Business," *The New Yorker* 20 and 27 October 1997.

Let me illustrate this with the example that I know best, that of my own university. Viadrina European University was set up in 1991 to serve as an academic link between Germany and Poland, as a bridge across a particularly troubled border. It has opened up its programs of study to students from Central and Eastern Europe, mainly Poland, but also the Ukraine, Russia, the Czech Republic, with the result that it now has the largest percentage of foreign students of any German university, including over a thousand students from Poland alone. Building this bridge through teaching and research has become the special mission, the special profile of the Viadrina, and it is imperative that its limited resources be geared to sustaining this profile as much as possible. It does not work perfectly by any means, but those projects that do conform to this profile, and particularly to our cooperation with Poland through the Collegium Polonicum on the other side of the Oder river, have a priority claim on the university's resources, especially those resources that it receives from the European Union (EU).

8. Funds and Fiefdoms: The Internal Distribution of Resources

In talking earlier about the level where funding decisions are made in the relationship between the state and the individual university, I have spoken of a contractual kind of agreement by which institutional goals and priorities become the basis for a funding formula and a funding commitment by the state. At the next stage of the allocation process, the distribution of resources inside an institution, we face a similar problem, but with somewhat different players. The problem is at this level exacerbated by the existence of what I have called "fiefdoms" inside the university – professorships, institutes, chairs – which have a tendency (a) to insist on the retention of previous funding commitments (invoking the principle of "Besitzstandswahrung" or preservation of acquired property rights), and (b) to watch carefully over the maintenance of parity in the allocation of resources. Here, as at the level of resource allocation to entire institutions, the only answer to the problem seems to lie in carefully negotiated agreements in which the level of funding is a function of the recipient's responsibilities and performance. Those agreements are not easy to obtain, but they are easier to obtain if the agreement is openly and transparently negotiated so that, for every participant in the process looking at every other participant, the correspondence between performance and load parameters and funding commitments is understandable. Without that kind of transparency, there is very little chance to succeed in the effort to make the allocation of resources more performance-oriented.

IV

Let me conclude by switching to a slightly different set of concerns. These concerns do not, except for the very last one, have directly to do with financing. Let me remind you, though, that in higher education, as in soccer, everything hangs together with everything else. As I look at higher education in the countries I know best, I am preoccupied by these broader issues as much as I am worried about how much my own university is going to lose or gain in next year's budget.

For the sake of brevity, let me state these final concerns in the form of three simple theses.

Thesis 1: *Institutions of higher education have a remarkable capacity for resisting change and reform.*

There are, to be sure, notable exceptions from this rule, and what is true for institutions of higher education is not necessarily true of systems of higher education, where political will from outside the universities has accomplished – for better or worse – a great deal of change in recent years. The United Kingdom, the Netherlands, Denmark and others serve as examples, and Germany may well be about to join the list.

Institutions of higher education, however, have a very hard time responding to new challenges. This may be particularly true of German universities – where even the unusual opportunity for reform that presented itself at the time of unification was passed up without as much as a ripple –, but I think it is true more generally. As I see it, this kind of institutional inertia has something to do with (1) a basic and essentially healthy skepticism of a professional organization towards new and untried departures, but also (2) with the extraordinarily important role of "property rights" among many of the principal actors in higher education, notably the faculty, and (3), as Gareth Williams points out[7] with the general difficulty of accomplishing change under the rather threatening conditions of resource scarcity, where every change is perceived as jeopardizing the advantages of the status quo even more seriously than it would under normal circumstances.

Thesis 2: *Higher education is increasingly facing a crisis of confidence with regard to its role and acceptance in society.*

---

[7]   Gareth Williams, "Finance and the Organisational Behaviour of Higher Education Institutions," *Towards Excellence in European Higher Education in the 90's (Proceedings of the 11th European AIR Forum, Trier, August 27-30, 1989)*, ed. Edgar Frackmann and Peter Maassen (Utrecht: Lemma, 1992) 89.

As I look at higher education in both the US and Germany, I am struck by how thoroughly the previously unassailable status of higher education in the society at large has been under siege in the last few decades, and how easily nitpicking congressmen or aggressive journalists and talkshow hosts get away with taking pot shots at higher education over questions of indirect cost recovery, undergraduate curricula, or affirmative action policies. Once taken for granted and serving as the basis for rather considerable privileges for the institution and its members, the social pre-eminence of higher education has come in for serious questioning and a consistent demand for greater transparency and accountability.

This is probably as it should be, and is moving things to a level of normality where higher education is put on a level with other social institutions, but it also affects quite significantly the future politics of higher education.

Thesis 3: *There is developing an uneasy competition between, on the one hand, securing the financial basis of higher education and, on the other, maintaining and strengthening its intellectual quality.*

This may not, or at least not yet, be the stuff that contradictions are made of, but there is no question in my mind that there is, in the situation that I have described in this paper, a danger of sacrificing the slow and steady growth of scholarly quality for short-term economic returns, and that the increasingly fierce competition for financial resources may place a heavy burden on the intellectual integrity of higher education institutions. This kind of tension very much bears watching.

WITTEN/HERDECKE UNIVERSITY – STILL (?) A SPECIAL CASE AMONG UNIVERSITIES IN GERMANY

Konrad SCHILY

In the context of our discussion of US American and German universities, my contribution will be a report on a special case in Germany, the private Witten/Herdecke University.

Witten/Herdecke received official state recognition in 1982, after a prolonged political tug-of-war. New legal regulations governing universities were passed in 1979, admitting for the first time universities outside state control, which had not existed in Germany before.

For Germans at that time, universities were only conceivable in connection with state control; the history of German universities over 600 years – if we start with the foundation of Heidelberg University and discount Prague – is mainly a history of state universities, or rather, of foundations by sovereigns and kings.

The foremost motives for kings or sovereigns was the wish to train their own experts in legal and financial matters, and in theology, and not to have to import them from Italy or France. An additional impulse was provided by the Reformation. Professional training, it was felt, should bear the mark of the correct theology, i.e. religious denomination.

A special case was the foundation of technical colleges at the end of the 19th century; first they were civil foundations strongly supported by the commercial sector; but soon the state authorities took charge of them. They also introduced fresh ideas into university education and resulted in a departure from mediaeval university concepts.

Konrad SCHILY: former President of the Private Universität Witten/Herdecke; Deputy Chairman of the Board of Trustees, Private Universität Witten/Herdecke; professionally specialized in neurology and psychiatry; former medical assignments at Frankfurt a. M., Berlin, Ebersberg/Munich, Tübingen, Herdecke, and Langenfeld; he has launched the program for musical therapy at the Musikhochschule Aachen in coorporation with the Herdecke hospital.

Another exception from the rule was the university at Frankfurt/Main, founded mainly with Jewish capital at the turn of the last century; however, inflation and the world-wide economic crisis soon turned it into just another state-controlled university. As to contents and organization, no progress was to be noted.

Consequently, 600 years of German university history represent state control, and 200 of these – from 1810 onwards – constitute the history of Prussian universities.

It is not correct to connect the history of Prussia's universities with the name of Wilhelm von Humboldt, as happens quite often. The Prussian university reform was considerably influenced by German Idealism and humanistic Enlightenment; but it was by no means what Wilhelm von Humboldt had in mind; otherwise he would certainly not have given up his position in the ministry of the Prussian state after only one year.

Wilhelm von Humboldt took the view that "without the state, things are far better," as he had stated in his important essay "Ideas on a Study to Determine the Limits of State Efficiency." Wilhelm von Humboldt did not wish for "the spirit of the government to prevail in any such institution," even be it wise and beneficial; this would only result in "uniformity and a strange conduct of the nation."

> People, instead of entering into social contact to sharpen their powers – even if thereby they might lose exclusive possession and benefits – would rather achieve possessions at the expense of their powers. It is precisely this diversity, resulting from the concourse of many, which constitutes the greatest good in society; and this diversity will certainly be lost inasmuch as the state intervenes. No longer do the members of a nation form a society; instead, individual subjects enter into a relationship with the state, i.e. with the spirit prevailing in its government; in this relationship, the superior powers of the state will restrain a free play of forces. Uniform causes have uniform effects. The more the state intervenes, the higher the uniformity of acting forces and their results. And this is precisely what the states intend. They want prosperity and peace; and both are easier to achieve if there is less conflict between individual competing views. [1]

The truly damaging effect is therefore that state institutions "weaken the power of a nation"; "he who is often and much directed, will easily reach a condition where he willingly gives up what remains of his independence."

We should therefore rather speak of the Prussian university reform. One positive aspect was that, in the second half of the 19th century, also and in

---

[1]   Wilhelm von Humboldt: *Ideen zu einem Versuch, die Grenzen der Wirksamkeit des Staates zu bestimmen* (Stuttgart: Reclam, 1967) 30f.

particular natural scientists gained the status of civil servants and thus financial security for themselves and their dependants; this meant they could actually concentrate on research. Secured income, provision for children and widows, performance orientation and a small degree of bureaucracy were beneficial characteristics of the Prussian university reform.

In the United States, however, Humboldt's reform concepts found a fertile soil. In Germany the fact is mainly unknown that one of the first universities to be founded in the United States on the basis of Humboldt's concept is Johns Hopkins University in Baltimore. The conversion of Harvard College into Harvard University also followed the example of the Berlin foundation, and in the last analysis Harvard University has become a role model for modern American universities, also for the state-controlled universities in the Middle West and California.

Humboldt was taken far more seriously in America than ever in Germany. US Americans also had a more pronounced distrust of their own state, or of any state, since many of them had emigrated to the United States not for reasons of economic need but because they had been persecuted in and by the states of the 18th and 19th century because of their social views, religious denomination, language or political affiliation. In the new country, they maintained a healthy distrust of the state, and more self-confidence. They knew, "things go better without the state."

An article written by Steven Muller in 1985 as president of Johns Hopkins University, entitled "Wilhelm von Humboldt and the University in the United States," ends with the following remark: "What could be more paradoxical than the fact that a heroic effort to reshape Prussian education along the lines of a classical Greek tradition, which was more imaginary than real, should have led so directly to the creation in America of precisely the right new university for the new industrial and technological age?" [2]

An essay by Helmut F. Spinner entitled "The Althoff System and Max Weber's Criticism" points out that the ideas propagated in 1809 were not only imitated, but also stimulated parallel developments. For Helmut F. Spinner, the foundation of the Prussian general staff from 1807 onwards was a reformative work, starting almost simultaneously, as an attempt to institutionalize military excellence and thus was an almost like-minded parallel activity and of equal importance in its international consequences.

---

[2]   Qtd. in Manfred Eigen: "Die deutsche Universität," *Die Idee der Universität: Versuch einer Standortbestimmung* (Berlin: Springer, 1988) 84.

According to Spinner, "Humboldt's legacy may be compared to that of Scharnhorst. Both result in the foundation of new institutions, in favor of an unbureaucratic spirit in research, or in warfare. In both cases, a unique milieu emerged for those who were to study the pertinent problems and find ways to solve them." [3]

At the beginning of the 19th century, Prussia proceeded to become a state administrating cultural affairs, with unbureaucratic and performance-oriented methods. This performance orientation, in the form of elevated examination standards – always geared to official requirements, of course – had also been introduced into the secondary school or grammar-school system; one of the consequences was that these schools, so far mainly a haven of the educated middle classes, were increasingly opened to the lower classes on the basis of performance. The percentage of pupils from the lower ranks of society increased up to 50 % of the total number of students.

The introduction of performance orientation in the military and the educational field was also directed against the dominance of the hierarchy of classes. Now it became possible to reach high military rank, or a professorship, not only on the basis of high birth or family connections, but also by acquiring the relevant diplomas, i.e. for members of the lower classes. Both systems underwent considerable alterations, also in their mutual relation. The educational institutions experienced more sweeping social changes, since the diploma system now made the position of scientists, or scholars, far more important. It was now possible to decide at the university whether to choose a military career, and what sort of.

According to Hans Ulrich Wehler, the state's sovereignty in the educational sector, through these official activities in the reform decade up to 1819, was extended so consistently that the idea of the state as the administrator of education could prevail in Prussia.

> From then on, the educational bureaucracy not only controlled the school system up to the universities, it also gained sovereignty over educational institutions, with the right to determine the type of institutions and to regulate teaching at schools – as to curriculum, contents and methods – and at universities via faculty classification, denomination of chairs, foundation of seminars and institutes; the same applied to the general system of examinations for pupils, students, teachers and professors. The reform period also had paradoxical traits: In 1792, Humboldt passionately advocated individual and corporate autonomy and wished to limit state activities to the guaranteeing of external and internal security only, in an

---

[3]   Bernhard von Brocke, ed., *Wissenschaftsgeschichte und Wissenschaftspolitik im Industriezeitalter: Das "System Althoff" in historischer Perspektive*, (Hildesheim: Lax, 1991).

effort to determine limits to state efficiency, and thus made a name for himself as one of the first strictly individualistic, even fanatically liberal theorists in Germany. On the other hand, in political practise he contributed rigorously to what he himself had called the worst and most oppressive despotism, i.e. to extend state sovereignty – far beyond its traditional duties – to the educational sector[4].

One of the immediate consequences of the state-controlled, three-tier educational system, i.e. primary and secondary schools and the universities, was a strict separation in teacher training, with different types of final exams and qualifications. The primary school teacher attended a teacher seminary and remained at the primary school for the rest of his active career. The secondary school teacher concluded his curriculum at a faculty of humanities, passed a state examination and taught at a secondary or grammar school. A professor took his doctorate at a faculty – in 1816, the post-doctoral university lecturing qualification, or habilitation, as we say in German, was added as a second academic requirement – and then was active in teaching and research at the university to which he had received a call. All people professionally involved in teaching were civil servants under public law. Despite strict separation into ranks and income groups, privileges and duties, these three new types of teachers had one thing in common: absolute dependence on the state.

Prussia played a leading political role in the unification of the German Reich, just as its educational system was to be adopted later by the united German Reich. This in mind one can understand that the next decisive turning-point in the history of German universities was 1933 when the national socialists came into power. The universities, all under state control, were purged from politically and racially undesirable elements. In March or April of 1933, a civil service law was passed for this purpose. By November of the same year, all universities reported "mission completed." The Humboldt University in Berlin lost 38 % of its teachers in the process, and certainly not the least capable ones.

We come to 1968, and to the so-called student revolt. Everything remained under state control. Prussia had contributed to some decrease in bureaucracy. Now, bureaucracy was strengthened with a vengeance, and democracy integrated. This removed the only chance of originality, and of unexpected excellence. The old university of "professors in ordinary" was replaced by the group university. Performance orientation disappeared for many years from universities. This is why the then president of Germany, von Weizsäcker, said on the occasion of the 600th anniversary of Heidelberg University: "The only winner in the 68 revolution was state administration."

---

[4]   Hans-Ulrich Wehler: *Deutsche Gesellschaftsgeschichte*, Vol. 1, (München: Beck, 1987).

I have provided such a long and detailed introduction as background information for the objectives behind the foundation of Witten/Herdecke University. The actual background at that time was the "collapse" of the German university system.

Witten/Herdecke University today still stands for the ideal of a free, responsible community of teachers and students. It is this humanistic spirit, and also the tradition of German or rather Central European Idealism which Witten/Herdecke subscribes to. Hence, the intention to found a private university as the only lawful way in Germany to evade state control. Actually we are a public university, but at our own responsibility. The step of privatization did not mean a step away from the state and a step towards the business sector, but rather in the direction of independence and responsibility towards society.

Not in the direction of the business sector! This was also the reason why Witten/Herdecke was not founded as a one-department structure; instead, a variety of disciplines and faculties were scheduled from the beginning. Today these are the faculties of:

medicine *(Dr. med.* = M.D. or medical doctor; *Dr. rer. nat.* = D.Sc. or doctor of natural sciences)

- training as a physician, approbation
- music therapy, diploma as a music therapist
- nursing science, and Bachelor or Master of Nursing

dental medicine or **dentistry** *(Dr. med. dent.* = doctor of dentistry)

natural sciences *(Dr. rer. nat.* = D. Sc. or doctor of natural sciences)

- biochemistry (diploma as a biochemist)
- environmental engineering (Dr.-Ing. = doctorate in engineering)

economics (diploma or doctorate)

liberal arts *(Dr. phil.* = Ph. D.)

Some general remarks on study courses at Witten/Herdecke University:

We select our students via comprehensive selection procedures. The individual faculties are responsible for selection. The aim of these procedures is to find capable, independent, performance-oriented and responsible students. We are looking for personality and try to discover it in these young people. The actual grades of the school-leaving certificate *(Abitur)* are not very important; our interviewers don't even know these results. But we have to register the

Abitur record and to consider it up to a certain point, since admission at state universities for some disciplines, like medicine, requires a certain standard of performance at school, and we have to meet the same standards in this respect.

Practically speaking, we receive applications in writing; two persons for each case have to agree whether to send out an invitation for interviews or not. The interview day then decides on acceptance. Depending on faculties, applicants meet between six and nine different interviewers, who at the end of the day have to accept or to turn down an applicant on the basis of a unanimous decision.

This preselection is important; our students are not expected to continue the ways of school at our university, but to independently acquire knowledge and skills of the discipline they select.

In the course of their studies, they are expected to demonstrate their ability to get around in international contexts, and in addition to their own disciplines to discover fields of special interest for independent studies.

This means:

– All disciplines involve practical work from the beginning. In medicine, students are employed in outpatient wards or hospitals; students of dentistry assist in dental treatment of patients; students of economics work in mentor companies (each student enters into an agreement on the type of cooperation with a mentor company six weeks after enrolment).
– All students are expected to acquire academic and practical qualifications in their own field, and in addition to study aspects of history, literature, philosophy and the rest of the humanities. Fundamental studies offer a variety of lectures and events for this purpose.

The overriding concept in all this is as much freedom and individual responsibility as possible. State administration urges for comparability and thus uniformity. We aim at original, individual solutions. This is why our students are free to select a foreign country or an institution there for practical work. We do not impose instructions on mentor companies; we only urge for a fruitful cooperation between both sides (student and mentor company alike). There is no fixed curriculum or conformity in fundamental studies, only the ever-present challenge to perform.

This principle of individual responsibility applies to the curricula but also to the organization as such. The university is an independent business enterprise in the legal form of a limited liability company.

The university sets its own objectives and is fully independent as to finances and personnel, and as to all legal transactions in its own right.

Structure of Witten/Herdecke University

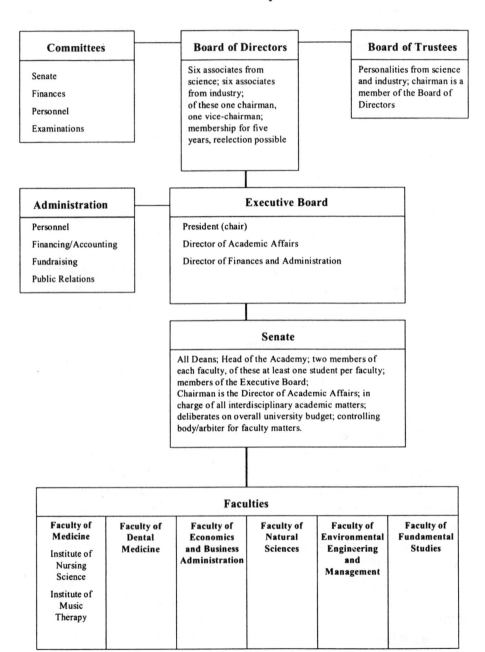

Committees

Senate

Finances

Personnel

Examinations

Board of Directors

Six associates from science; six associates from industry; of these one chairman, one vice-chairman; membership for five years, reelection possible

Board of Trustees

Personalities from science and industry; chairman is a member of the Board of Directors

Administration

Personnel

Financing/Accounting

Fundraising

Public Relations

Executive Board

President (chair)

Director of Academic Affairs

Director of Finances and Administration

Senate

All Deans; Head of the Academy; two members of each faculty, of these at least one student per faculty; members of the Executive Board; Chairman is the Director of Academic Affairs; in charge of all interdisciplinary academic matters; deliberates on overall university budget; controlling body/arbiter for faculty matters.

Faculties

Faculty of Medicine	Faculty of Dental Medicine	Faculty of Economics and Business Administration	Faculty of Natural Sciences	Faculty of Environmental Engineering and Management	Faculty of Fundamental Studies
Institute of Nursing Science					
Institute of Music Therapy					

This means that we are not only responsible for our own failures, but also that we may learn from them. In new situations we have a chance to put our own solutions to the test.

This legal independence and the resulting challenging potential of freedom and responsibilities has generated our own brand of creativity which has made Witten/Herdecke University a success.

Even with state recognition in 1982, all was not going as well as we might have wished for. We had to promise not to demand fees; financial subsidies out of public funds were ruled out "permanently"; as we could not present any property assets, we had to deposit with the government of the state of Nordrhein-Westfalen (NRW) securities of a leading German banking house amounting to 17 million DM, on a rotating revolving basis for 5 years in advance.

We accepted these preconditions in order to start. We had to swallow these "toads" (as we say it in German) but did not digest them. Meanwhile we have been able to return all of them.

From 1983 to 1991, we financed expenditures exclusively from donations, income from research projects etc. In 1989, a first contract was signed with the NRW government on investment moneys for university buildings; after an evaluation by the federal government's *Wissenschaftsrat* (Science Council), the sum was doubled out of federal funds (25 million DM from NRW, and 25 million DM from the federal government).

In 1994, we made it clear to the NRW government that continued financing exclusively from donations and income from research projects was no longer feasible; our donors were no longer willing to accept that the NRW government would not subsidize a model university of international reputation, nor that students did not pay anything for a university education which demonstrably resulted in better training and also in better job opportunities afterwards.

I am not going to expatiate upon the details of the subsequent political altercations with the then Minister of Science and Research; we had touched upon taboos (student fees are anti-social; a private institution must not benefit from public funds).

But let me present a short outline of our solution for tuition – a payment scheme which was mainly designed by our students. Before, however, I will demonstrate that the introduction of fees has not changed the composition of students in terms of social background.

Expenditures at Witten/Herdecke University
1981-1998

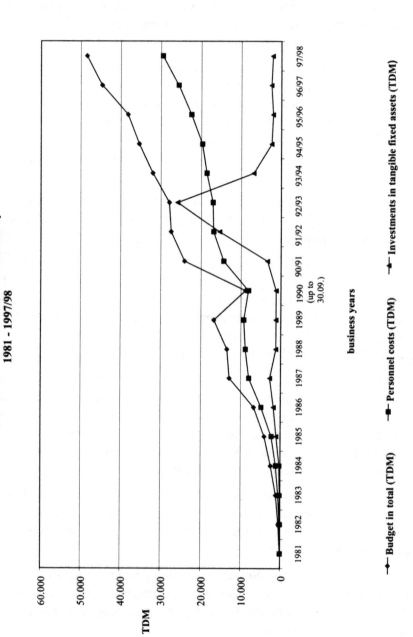

Data on scholarships for highly gifted students

Financing of students in the winter term 1997/98	
	%
Recipients of BAföG (nation-wide scholarship system)	21,8
other scholarship holders	7,2
total	29

Scholarship organizations for highly gifted students without doctorates (as per November 1997)	
Studienstiftung des deutschen Volkes	28
Friedrich Naumann Stiftung	13
Evangelisches Studienwerk Villigst	7
Cusanuswerk Deutschland	5
Friedrich Ebert Stiftung	3
Konrad Adenauer Stiftung	3
Hans Böckler Stiftung	3
Hanns Seidel Stiftung	3
Heinrich Böll Stiftung	1
total	66

28 students of Witten/Herdecke University are recipients of scholarships of Studienstiftung des Deutschen Volkes, which places Witten/Herdecke University at No. 2 of all German universities (as per November 1997).

When I explained to our students in 1994 that we could not continue without a financial contribution on their part, they were not happy. But they accepted the situation and cooperated to develop a sound and viable payment system.

- We have so far not demanded money from students upon admittance, and intend to leave it at that.
- Costs are not to have a regulative or controlling influence upon the curriculum.
- We do not want to fix fees per discipline; e.g. medical curriculum = expensive, or economics = less expensive.
- Students who opt for payment advance on the basis of a loan are to graduate without a fixed amount of debts incurred, in order to feel free to select a job of their own choice. (If debts to banks are too high, graduates cannot choose jobs in research or the social welfare sector, where incomes tend to be low.)

The following measures help to solve the problems:

- The foundation of a student association or "StudierendenGesellschaft." This is a non-profit financing organization owned by our students; they are not concerned with the social background of a student but differentiate between three different types of payment, i.e. fees to be paid either after graduation, or over the course of studies, or a mixture of both.
- In the case of payment advance on the basis of a loan, a student signs a contract under which after graduation and after starting in a salaried job he/she will pay 8 % of his/her income to the StudierendenGesellschaft for eight years. As soon as the sums returned reach a ceiling of DM 45.000,-, even before the eight years are over, payments can stop.
- For all major and postgraduate or specialized study courses, a fee has been determined according to the number of terms or semesters involved.
- Costs for a major study course amount to approximately DM 30.000,-. For a medical curriculum, the usual study period of six years means an annual contribution of DM 5.000,-, or DM 450,- per month. The total sum remains the same, even if a student should spend 1 1/2 additional years in China, e.g., or if for some reason or other, such as additional courses of a certain length, he or she should need more time; only the fixed sum for the regular period of studies applies.
- The StudierendenGesellschaft acts as a business partner for the university; i.e. they agree per contract to pay such and such a sum in DM to the university over the regular study course, so that we look at a triangle here: the student has a contract with his StudierendenGesellschaft, a different, mainly academic contract with the university, and the StudierendenGesellschaft and the university are connected by another contract.

Let me summarize. Witten/Herdecke continues in the best tradition of European Enlightenment, when students achieved academic freedom. We are looking for independence. We aim at individual solutions in science, in teaching, and of course in the curriculum. We attach importance to the fact that today a variety of practice-oriented professions require university training; this idea was still inconceivable at the beginning of the 19th century and therefore goes beyond Humboldt: our main objectives are these idealistic liberties and responsibilities. On the economic and financial side, we endeavor to maintain efficient business-like standards and therefore have introduced a corresponding planning and report system. The following charts are to demonstrate this policy. The practical business side, however, is only a means to an end, just as legal independence is only another means to an end. The end is in fact a continuation of Enlightenment; and since we are concerned with young people, this means encounters within one generation and between generations, within one civilization and between civilizations.

It is my firm conviction that this is going to be an essential part of the mission of universities in the future: a true conceptual globalization, i.e. a far-reaching comprehensive connection with other civilizations, and simultaneously, a cultivation of our own roots. This could be the great chance for Europe; no centralization nor – even worse – more bureaucracy, but rather a lively exchange on the basis of cultural diversity in Europe.

UNIVERSITY HISTORY

1980	Universitätsverein Witten/Herdecke e. V. was founded
1982	Recognition of the private Witten/Herdecke University by the Federal Government
1983	The Faculty of Medicine was opened
1984	Study courses in economics and dental medicine followed
1985	Postgraduate study course in Music Therapy
1987	Natural sciences, major study course in biochemistry
	All business and other activities were transferred from the founding body (Universitätsverein) to the non-profit limited liability company, Private Universität Witten/Herdecke GmbH
1989	End of the actual developmental stage: Contract between Witten/Herdecke University, the NRW Government and the Bertelsmann Foundation with the objective to ensure quality in research and teaching at Witten/Herdecke University and to further expand its faculties
1990	The Science Council (Federal Government) reviews the university, which as a result is accepted into the list of universities to be subsidized according to regulations on public funds for university buildings
1991 – 1993	Planning and construction of the central campus building
1993	The Institute of Fundamental Studies achieves faculty status
	The university moves into the new central campus building
1996	The Science Council again reviews the university and in its evaluation underlines the exceptional model character of Witten/Herdecke. In compliance with its recommendations, the NRW Government agrees to support Witten/Herdecke University with public funds
	Introduction of curricula of Nursing Science, Pharmaceutical Medicine (postgraduate course), Traditional Chinese Medicine (further education) and Techniques and Management in the Construction and Facilities Industries (specialized complementary course)

NUMBER OF STUDENTS AND APPLICANTS

Number of students per faculty and types of graduation (WS 1995/96 bis WS 1997/98)			
Faculty	WS 95/96	WS 96/97	WS 97/98
Natural Science and Environmental Engineering and Management		68	59
Biochemistry (diploma)	69	7	7
further education: Building Trade	3		
Economics (diploma in economics)	233	251	277
Medicine			
state examination in medicine	217	242	256
diploma in music therapy	12	13	10
nursing science		53	86
postgraduate course in pharmaceutical medicine			20
Dental medicine			
state examination in dental medicine	151	168	179
Studium fundamentale			
doctorates	13	11	17
total	698	813	911

Prospective development in number of students 1998/99 through 2002/03					
Faculty	1998/99	1999/00	2000/01	2001/02	2002/03
Natural science	35	40	50	60	60
Economics	250	270	290	320	350
Medicine	270	270	270	270	270
Music Therapy	10	10	10	10	10
Nursing Science	100	130	160	190	210
Dental Medicine	150	150	150	150	150
Students (excl. doctorates)	815	870	930	1.000	1.050
doctorates (enrolled)	110	120	130	140	150
total number of students	925	990	1.060	1.140	1.200
prospective student fees (million DM)	2,8	3,1	3,4	3,7	4,0

Income Statement
1 October 1997 until 30 September 1998
(Short Version)

	TDM
Income from donations and foundations	17,079
Income from appropriated contributions	1,250
Income from research subsidies	7,083
Income from clinic of dentistry	6,568
Income from state government subsidies	10,500
Income from tuition fees	2,594
Other operational income	4,971
Total income	**50,045**
Personnel expenses	29,555
Costs of materials clinic of dentistry	2,910
Depreciation on fixed assets	3,231
Other operational expenses	12,699
Total expenses	**48,395**
Financial result	**-378**
Profit for the year (before obligatory provision for reserves)	1,272
Profit brought forward	1,530
Withdrawals from appropriated reserves	254
Provision for appropriated reserves	-1,250
Unappropriated retained earnings	**1,806**

WITTEN/HERDECKE UNIVERSITY

**Balance Sheet
as of 30 September 1998
(Short Version)**

ASSETS	TDM
Fixed Assets	
Intangible assets	694
Land, buildings	36,208
Furniture and fixtures	5,356
Financial assets	49
Subtotal	*42,307*
Current Assets	
Inventories	928
Accounts receivable	1,232
Other assets	14,543
Cash	1,137
Subtotal	*17,840*
Prepaid Expenses	276
Total Assets	***60,423***

LIABILITIES	TDM
Equity	
Share capital	60
Appropriated reserves	9,548
Unappropriated retained earnings	1,806
Subtotal	*11,414*
Separate Item for Investment Subsidies	35,582
Provisions	4,637
Liabilities	
Accounts payable	1,389
Other liabilities	2,611
Subtotal	*4,000*
Deferred Income	4,790
Total Liabilities	***60,423***

Financial scope for the business years 1998/99 through 2002/03 (in million DM)					
Type of financing	1997/98	1998/99	1999/00	2000/01	2001/02
donations and foundations	17,2	16,9	17,4	16,7	17,7
– of these, pledged / guaranteed	16,7	15,9	15,9	11,7	11,1
– probably renewed				2,5	3,1
– to be raised anew	0,5	1,0	1,5	2,5	3,5
research funds (external financing and donations for research)	8,1	8,4	8,7	9,0	9,3
income from services rendered (incl. returns of dental clinic)	6,4	6,6	6,8	7,0	7,2
tuition	2,8	3,1	3,4	3,7	4,0
subsidies from NRW government	10,0	10,0	10,0	10,0	10,0
total income	44,5	45,0	46,3	46,4	48,2

DIFFERENTIATION BY ROLE AND MISSION OF INSTITUTIONS OF HIGHER EDUCATION IN THE UNITED STATES

Daniel FALLON

Higher education in the United States has developed over a period of more than 300 years in a loosely uncoordinated fashion. It has been influenced by local events, political struggles, and economic expansion. It is occasionally referred to as a "system," although that word, in my opinion, still implies more order and coherence than actually exists. Nonetheless, the forces of economic integration and an emerging new economy are increasingly pushing formerly disparate elements together, and the idea of a system of higher education in the United States is becoming more plausible. As we now enter an era of mass higher education, our history has bequeathed to us a remarkably diverse array of institutions serving many different kinds of students and performing many distinctively different functions. Fortunately, such a highly differentiated structure is well suited to an economy generating new wealth largely through knowledge and information and requiring most of its citizens to attain significant postsecondary education.

Individual institutions of higher education in the United States are largely understood today to be functioning within understandable categories. We call the most important and clearest of these categories the role and mission of an institution. Another distinguishing characteristic that we can easily recognize is independent of these categories. It is the locus of control of the institution, which can be public, private, or proprietary. Because a distinction based upon locus of control is so prevalent in the United States, and so rare in Europe, it will be useful to be clear about what these differences actually mean.

Daniel FALLON: Professor of Psychology and Professor of Public Affairs at the University of Maryland, College Park where he was Vice President for Academic Affairs and Provost; former Professor of Psychology at Texas A&M University, at the New York State University at Binghamton, and at the University of Colorado at Denver; trained as an experimental psychologist, he has contributed to the scientific literature on the study of learning and motivation, for instance his prize-winning book *The German University*.

"Public" means largely dependent upon legislatively appropriated tax funds and governed by a board appointed by publicly elected officials. "Private" means largely dependent upon income from charitable trusts and from fees paid by students, and governed by a board that is usually self-perpetuating with minimal public oversight. Both public and private institutions of higher education are nonprofit organizations that exist only for the purpose of education and return no profits. "Proprietary," in contrast, means largely dependent upon income from the sale of educational services and governed by a board, often responsible to stockholders, which demands a profit returned upon investment.

We should begin our discussion by considering what is meant by the concept of "public" and "private" universities in the United States. This has been a topic of considerable fascination, and much fantasy, for German observers. One common stereotype encountered with high frequency in German public media, and in general discussion, is that the truly excellent universities in the United States are private universities that charge high tuition and are thus accessible almost exclusively to a wealthy elite. Public universities, in contrast, are often regarded as facing the same problems of quantity and quality as German universities. This misconception has little basis in current or historical fact and is a significant impediment to serious crossnational consideration of higher education issues.

We should remember that in 1809, when Wilhelm von Humboldt conceived the academic design for the University of Berlin, there was no distinction between public and private universities in the United States. Thomas Jefferson viewed the University of Virginia as competitor in every way to his own *alma mater*, the College of William & Mary, which in those days operated in Virginia just as Harvard did in Massachusetts. Harvard University had from the 17th century been supported heavily by tax revenues from the State of Massachusetts and was widely regarded as the Massachusetts university, just as Yale was considered the university for Connecticut, and was accordingly supported by the taxpayers of its state. This situation changed abruptly as a result of a quarrel between the president of Dartmouth College in New Hampshire and the trustees of that institution.

Dartmouth College had been founded, with assistance of the governor general of the colony of New Hampshire, by Eleazer Wheelock, in 1769. It obtained its charter from King George III. By the early nineteenth century, Eleazer's son, John Wheelock, had become president, and was a reformer with modern ideas. The trustees, however, had become increasingly conservative and were alarmed by John Wheelock's views on religion and by his interest in modern languages and practical subjects such as agriculture. The quarrel became acute when the trustees fired President Wheelock, who took his case to the governor, the state legislature, and the people of New Hampshire.

The elections of 1816 were decided on the basis of the Dartmouth College issue, and President Wheelock's supporters won a resounding victory, attaining a majority in the legislature and a sympathetic new governor. The legislature quickly voted to change the name of the institution to Dartmouth University, to fire the Board of Trustees, and to re-install John Wheelock as president. The trustees sued. Everyone felt that their case was weak, since it depended essentially upon an argument that their charter existed before there was a State of New Hampshire, and, therefore, the State could exert no control over them. The trustees' suit was denied by a unanimous decision of the supreme court of New Hampshire, which, in its opinion, advised the trustees not to waste money in an appeal of so weak and trivial a case.

Undaunted, the trustees took their case to the United States Supreme Court. The State of New Hampshire committed a strategic error at this point by not sending its best and most informed lawyers, but instead relying on hired attorneys in Washington, who did not represent them well. The trustees were represented by a young alumnus of Dartmouth College, Daniel Webster, who was at that time just beginning his career. Later he went on to become a distinguished U.S. Senator and is today recognized as one of the greatest orators and legislators in the history of the United States. Webster's summation to the court was brilliant, and moved both himself and Chief Justice John Marshall to tears at its conclusion.

Surprisingly in 1819 the United States Supreme Court ruled that Dartmouth College was not subservient to the state of New Hampshire and could not be forced by the state to offer certain courses of instruction. This was a radical ruling by a court, led by Chief Justice Marshall, still trying to sort out the implications of the American revolution. The decision was in keeping with a string of rulings that sought to reinforce principles of private property and private contracts within a democratic governmental system. It created the legal foundation for private colleges and universities in the United States.

At least in part because the Court's ruling was confusing to a nation that had not distinguished private from public institutions, it had little immediate effect. Dartmouth, Harvard, Yale, and similar institutions continued for many years to function as if they were public institutions and to receive state tax appropriations as part of their budgets. It was not until the time of the Civil War that higher education began to cohere into a recognizable pattern of public and private institutions. The U.S. Congress approved the Land-Grant Act of 1862, which provided federal public support for the establishment of state-based comprehensive universities. Shortly thereafter, the newly appointed president of Harvard University, Charles W. Eliot, argued that legislative influence in the affairs of a university was detrimental to its academic development, and began to sever most of Harvard's formal relationships with the State of Massachusetts. Most institutions with private charters followed Harvard's lead. In this climate, new foundings of colleges and universities began to take place under private auspices.

One might assume that if universities were private, they would be free to pursue any policy they pleased, including, for example, admitting only students from the upper classes, whose parents could afford to pay high tuition. The legacy of two hundred years of the public trust is not so easily put aside, however, and the older institutions, such as Harvard and Yale, continued to act as responsible public agencies. Furthermore, by the time of the second world war a heightened sense of democratic responsibility led these institutions to admit a broadly representative student body. In fact, since 1945 most "private" universities in the United States have pursued a strict policy of need-blind admission, in which applicants are admitted exclusively on academic merit, and financial aid is then applied to ensure that every student who is admitted may attend, regardless of family income. Furthermore, since 1945 the policies of the federal government have resulted in significant public financing of private universities, almost all of which also receive additional financial support from the governments of the states in which they are located.

At the same time, "public" universities have since 1970 become increasingly less dependent upon financial support from the states that created them, and receive today on average less than one-third of their annual budgets from legislatively appropriated tax dollars. Virtually all public universities now charge significant fees (tuition) collected directly from students. Some private universities charge low tuition, and some public universities charge high tuition. There are outstanding universities of the highest academic excellence in private and public sectors, just as there are also mediocre universities in both.

The financing of higher education in the United States is surprisingly similar for both private and public universities, and everywhere includes a mix of funds from four sources: (a) federal government; (b) state government; (c) the student; and (d) private contributions from individual philanthropists, charitable foundations, and business or industry. In short, the distinction between public and private universities in the United States, although real, is not profound. It has provided private institutions with somewhat greater flexibility and in some cases with greater wealth. Public and private institutions, however, serve similar students in similar ways, are financed by similar sources, and perform similar functions, just as they did at the founding of the United States.

Proprietary institutions are different from public and private universities in that they are operated as businesses. They developed in the late nineteenth century, primarily as vocational schools to train students for careers in accounting or secretarial work. By providing certificates of accomplishment, they enabled their graduates to obtain secure well-paying jobs. Because they were developed as training institutes rather than educational academies, their faculty were comprised largely of practitioners and they were supported almost exclusively from fees paid by students. By managing the enterprise well, the owners of such colleges could pay themselves good salaries and return profits in the form of bonuses and dividends. Today, such "for profit" institutions continue to exist, but are dominated by trades such as cosmetology, or culinary science, or morticianship. In the postwar period, a few significant comprehensive universities have emerged in this arena. They are highly profitable organizations, and shares in their corporations are traded on the New York Stock Exchange. Examples include the University of Phoenix, headquartered in Arizona, and the DeVries Institute, headquartered in Illinois. They focus on teaching, generally do no research, and do not award the Ph.D. degree. Their faculty, however, hold Ph.D. degrees, and teach across all disciplines. These institutions are very responsive to their students, value high quality teaching, strive to meet generally acknowledged standards of academic quality, are accredited, and award academic degrees. They represent at the moment a very small component in the mix of higher education in the United States.

Now, let's take a look at the distribution of institutions and students among these three sectors of higher education in the United States, by institutional control. Every year, the U.S. Office of Education assembles information on the enrollment of every student in every institution of higher education in the country. The most recent year for which I have a complete tally of the data is 1996. In that year, there were 6,849 institutions of higher education in the United States, and 15,107,632 students.

In this data set, which comes from the National Center for Education Statistics of the United States, an "institution of higher education" is defined broadly and thus encompasses the full variety of U.S. higher education. An institution is included in this data set if the U.S. federal government recognizes it as eligible to receive and distribute student aid from the national treasury. This means that these institutions matriculate only postsecondary students, are accredited by a federally-certified accrediting agency, and award a formal degree of some kind when a student completes the degree requirements.

Figure 1 presents the distribution of *institutions* by locus of control. One can see that, in terms of number of institutions, the distribution is evenly distributed among public, private, and proprietary. Indeed, there are more proprietary institutions than any other kind. What this figure does not show, however, is how many students are enrolled at each of these places. As one might expect, there are many very small proprietary institutions, and quite a few large public universities.

Figure 2 presents the distribution of *students* by locus of control. One can see here that only 4% of all students are enrolled in proprietary institutions, compared with 20% in private institutions. The overwhelming majority of students in the United States, 76%, are enrolled in public institutions.

Now let us consider the categories of higher education by role and mission of the institutions. The American design for higher education is highly dependent on an institution's role and mission. These roles and missions are most clearly understood by looking at the modern plan for the state of California, developed in the 1950's by the great American educational planner Clark Kerr. The premise in California is that every qualified student may obtain higher education at public expense. For those in the upper 12% of the ranks of secondary school graduates, as judged by grades and test scores, entry to a "research university" is permitted. For those in the upper 34%, entry to a "master's university" is permitted. And for all others, entry to a two-year "community college" is permitted. Each of these three types of higher education institution is said to have a distinctively different role and mission. Students distribute themselves among these three types of institution according to their convenience as well as their eligibility, so the actual percentages of students among the types is not the same as the eligibility criteria. Within California, there are today 9 research universities, 22 master's universities, and 108 two-year colleges, serving about two million students. About 8% of California students are enrolled in research universities, 18% in master's universities and 74% in two-year colleges.

I need to clarify what constitutes a university in the United States. Several institutions of higher education use the name "university" in their title, but that does not mean that they function as universities. To clarify these distinctions, an important philanthropic institution, the Carnegie Foundation for the Advancement of Teaching, has developed a classification scheme. The Carnegie Foundation separates institutions of higher education into several categories, of which only two are called "research universities." The institutions classified as research universities award a certain minimum number of doctoral degrees each year, in a certain minimum number of academic subjects, and they also receive a certain minimum amount of competitive research funding. It is only these research universities that are directly comparable to German universities. There are 125 of them in the United States, among a total of almost 7,000 institutions of higher education. These 125 research universities enroll about 18% of all higher education students in the United States.

The Carnegie classification scheme has become the standard way of describing the distribution of universities and colleges in the United States by their role and mission. Even though the Carnegie classification is the acknowledged standard, it is typical of higher education in the United States that this scheme was developed by a private philanthropy with no official governmental endorsement. Furthermore, the classification was developed relatively recently, in the twentieth century, and its purpose at first was simply to help observers make sense of a very confusing mix of institutions.

The current Carnegie classification scheme is shown in Table I. There are a total of ten categories of role and mission in the Carnegie classification, but several of these represent levels within a basic category. If one considers just the basic categories, there are six of them: research universities; doctoral universities; master's universities; bachelor's colleges; associate colleges; and specialized institutions.

Figure 3 presents the distribution of *institutions* by role and mission, as defined by the Carnegie classification. One can see here that virtually half of the institutions are "unclassified." These are predominately small proprietary institutions, such as beauty colleges, or schools of secretarial skills. Of the remainder, one can see that most institutions are two-year community colleges that award the associate degree, followed by four-year colleges, master's universities, doctoral universities, and research universities. Because of the disparity among the sizes of these institutions, just looking at the distribution of the number of institutions is misleading.

Figure 4 presents the distribution of *student enrollments* by role and mission, as defined by the Carnegie classification. Here one can easily see that, even though almost half of the institutions of higher education are unclassified, these unclassified schools are so small that they enroll only 6% of all of the students. As this figure shows, most students in the United States are enrolled at two-year community colleges (36%), followed next by the comprehensive masters-level institutions (21%), and then by the research universities (18%).

The distribution of students in institutions of higher education in the United States contrasts sharply with the distribution in the Federal Republic of Germany, where the postsecondary sector is dominated by what we would call in the United States the research university. The most recently available data for Germany that I was able to find in published form is in a publication of the Bundesministerium für Bildung, Wissenschaft, Forschung und Technologie, entitled *Higher Education in Germany*, by Hansgert Peisert and Gerhild Framhein. They come from a report of the Statistisches Bundesamt for enrollment in 1992.

Figure 5 presents the distribution of *institutions* by all of the various types that exist in the Federal Republic of Germany. Although many types are represented in this display, there are basically only three broad categories, each representing a different role and mission: research universities; specialized academies; and *Fachhochschulen*. Figure 5 shows just the number of institutions and overlooks the large differences in the size of the institutions.

Figure 6 presents the distribution of *student enrollments* by all types of institution. One can see here that enrollment of students in Germany is dominated by the traditional research universities. These relationships are easier to see if one collapses the categories into the basic three roles and missions.

Figure 7 presents the distribution of number of *institutions* of higher education in Germany by the three basic roles and missions.

Figure 8 presents the distribution of *student enrollments* by role and mission. Here, it is very clear that almost three-quarters of all German students are in enrolled in research universities in Germany.

The implications of a differentiated structure of higher education are many and important, and deserve detailed treatment in a separate analysis. For now, however, we can draw a few conclusions from the picture I have sketched.

First, the distinction in the United States of institutions by locus of control between private, public, and proprietary is of little practical policy significance. Most students are in public institutions, and there is considerable overlap in the financing and the function of public and private institutions. Proprietary institutions represent a negligible proportion of the total.

Second, it is clear that there is a high degree of differentiation in the United States, and very little in the Federal Republic of Germany. This is important for many reasons, but one obvious concern is that of cost. The most expensive form of education is that associated with the Ph.D. degree. It is the most significant contributor to the cost of higher education. In the United States, this form of education is limited to a very small number of institutions. In the Federal Republic of Germany it predominates.

Finally, the large number of relatively open-access institutions in the United States, particularly the two-year community colleges, facilitates the acquisition of postsecondary education for a large number of citizens. A highly educated citizenry is valuable for a modern economy, of course, but it also contributes to our sense of purpose in hoping to improve our civilization. I am reminded here of the founding period of our modern institutions, the time of Thomas Jefferson and of Wilhelm von Humboldt.

In 1791, at the age of 24, Wilhelm von Humboldt completed an essay to which he gave the title, "Ideen zu einem Versuch, die Grenzen der Wirksamkeit des Staates zu bestimmen." This piece was first known in English as "The Spheres and Duties of Government," and later as "The Limits of State Action." In it, Humboldt wrote:

> The grand leading principle, towards which every argument unfolded in these pages directly converges, is the absolute and essential importance of human development in its richest diversity.

This rich idea, which inspired John Stuart Mill's essay, "On Liberty," reminds us of the value of a broad and flexible array of institutions of higher education to serve a modern society.

Table I: Carnegie Classification Code Definitions

Research University I	Award at least 50 doctoral degrees each year Receive at least $40 million in federal research support
Research University II	Award at least 50 doctoral degrees each year Receive at least $15.5 million in federal research support
Doctoral I	Award at least 40 doctoral degrees each year, in at least five different disciplines
Doctoral II	Award at least 10 doctoral degrees each year, in at least three disciplines; or at least 20 doctoral degrees each year
Master's (Comprehensive) Colleges and Universities I	Award at least 40 master's degrees each year in at least three disciplines
Master's (Comprehensive) Colleges and Universities II	Award at least 20 master's degrees each year
Baccalaureate (Liberal Arts) Colleges I	Selective admissions; award at least 40% of bachelor's degrees in liberal arts disciplines
Baccalaureate Colleges II	Generally open admission, or less than 40% of bachelor's degrees in liberal arts disciplines
Associate of Arts Colleges	Award no baccalaureate degrees
Specialized Institutions	At least 50% of all degrees awarded are in a single specialized field

Figure 1
U.S. Institutions by Control

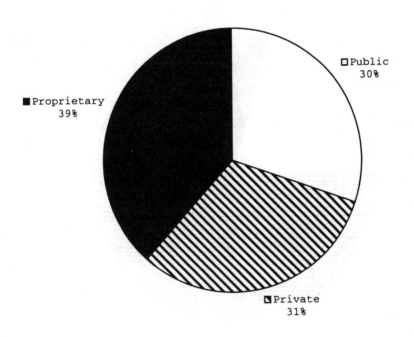

Figure 2
U.S. Enrollment by Control

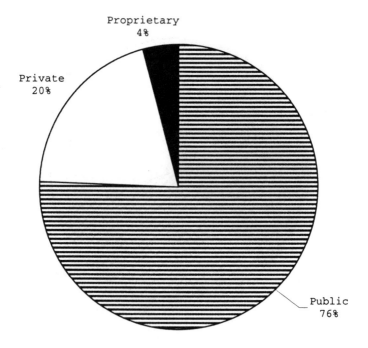

Figure 3
U.S. Institutions by Role and Mission

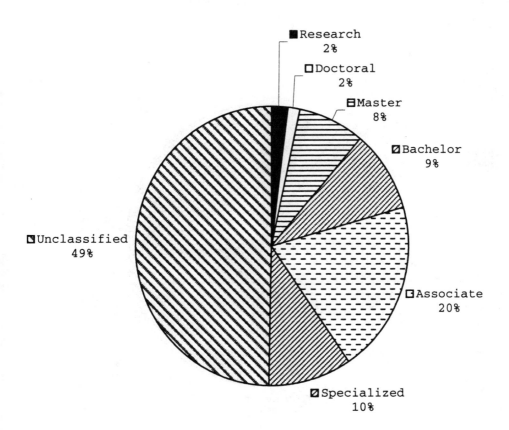

Figure 4
U.S. Enrollment by Role and Mission

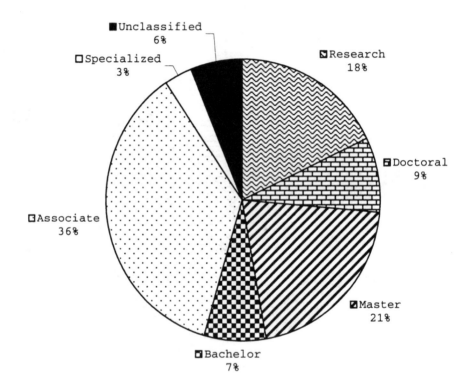

Figure 5
FRG Institutions by All Types

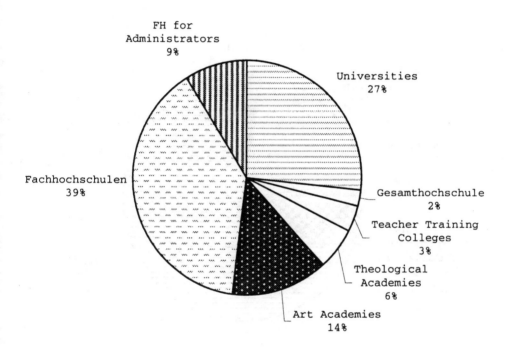

FH for
Administrators
9%

Universities
27%

Fachhochschulen
39%

Gesamthochschule
2%

Teacher Training
Colleges
3%

Theological
Academies
6%

Art Academies
14%

Figure 6
FRG Enrollment by All Types

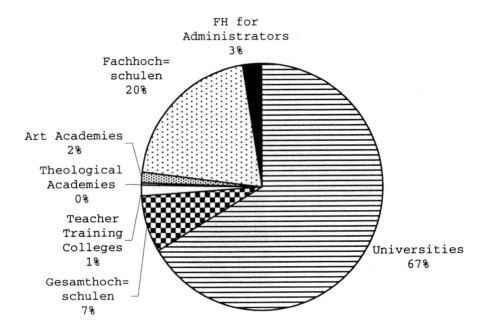

Figure 7
FRG Institutions by Role and Mission

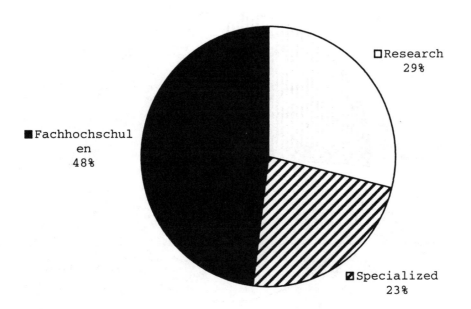

Figure 8
FRG Enrollment by Role and Mission

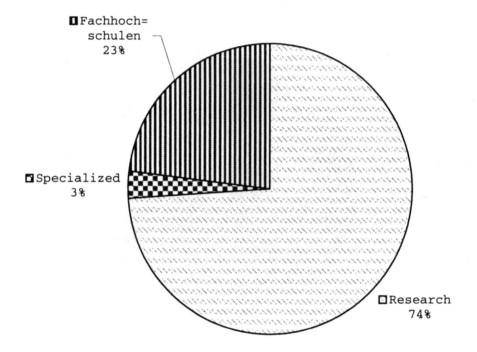

THE POSITION OF PART-TIME ADJUNCT VS. FULL TIME FACULTY AND THE ROLE OF THE AAUP

James PERLEY

The *American Association of University Professors* (AAUP) was founded in 1915 as a result of the firing of faculty members for extramural utterances found objectionable by those in administrative positions. The AAUP is an organization which includes all categories of faculty as long as they are involved in teaching and research, hence our members are from the entire range of institutions from Community Colleges to Research I Universities. We do not, however, have members from proprietary institutions. Among our founders were John Dewey and Arthur Lovejoy and the reasons for our birth were grounded in concerns about academic freedom and tenure. That work continues today. We have adopted the notion of censure to indicate that conditions violative of academic freedom exist at Colleges and Universities. Two recent examples of censure imposed by the AAUP may serve as examples of concerns that trigger censure. We recently censured the Minneapolis College of Art and Design over decisions made to entirely eliminate tenure of the faculty. A year after its elimination, virtually the entire tenured faculty was dismissed. This past year we censured Brigham Young University in Utah. A faculty member in the English Department was fired for her statement that she prayed to a Mother God in meetings off campus. Because many administrators were also church officials, this statement was seen as violative of the tenets of the church, sufficient to result in the termination of her employment.

James PERLEY: Danforth Professor of Biology at the College of Wooster, Ohio; he is a member of the American Association for the Advancement of Science, and the American Association of University Professors; former appointments include Wayne State University at Detroit, Michigan, Massay University at Palmerston North, New Zealand, the University of British Columbia at Vancouver, Canada, and the University of California at Berkeley; besides publications in the field of higher education, his research interests are the mechanism of action of plant growth hormones, biochemistry of auxin production, and inorganic nutrition of plants.

More recently, we have become involved in the area of governance and have assumed the right to issue sanctions for violation of traditional and commonly accepted standards of governance. We believe in the notion of collegial governance, which if honored respects the existence of greater responsibility of each component of the university in those areas where they have the greatest responsibility. Faculty members are regarded as having primary responsibility in the area of hiring of colleagues and in framing the curriculum, while members of Boards of Trustees have primary responsibility in seeing to the fiscal status of the institution. But more importantly, our views allow each segment of the community to have input into all areas of responsibility and we are firm in our belief that collegial governance creates the strongest institutions.

An example of a sanction imposed for violation of these standards occurred at Francis Marion University in South Carolina. There a new President, with the blessing of the Board of Trustees that appointed him, dismissed all elected standing faculty committees and replaced them with faculty members who agreed with his views. In addition to imposing sanctions, we continue to have concerns in developments which affect governance. Examples include recent developments in medical schools, and our report on Affirmative Action developments in the State of California. A Board of Review I empanelled examined the decision to abandon affirmative action standards in the California Universities and concluded Governor Wilson's decisions had been taken without the involvement of faculty as would have occurred if standards of collegial governance had been honored.

As one might imagine, our organization is full of committees and our practices are democratic. We have committees in every area where faculty members have interests. We have a Committee on Ethics, and another which deals with standards of accreditation. Still other committees deal with concerns of part time and adjunct faculty members, two-year colleges, and each year our *Committee on the Economic Standards of the Profession* issues a report on faculty salaries at institutions across the country. Our most recent efforts have involved an examination of Distance Learning and the development of a statement on intellectual property. Those concerned in Germany may want to watch for the appearance of these statements as they may well prove to be useful in Europe. When I received the list of concerns to be addressed at this conference, I was attracted immediately to the topic of professors and teaching staff, since my professional concerns over the past several years have centered on developments affecting faculty members.

I should like to give a short account of myself and my professional involvements. Understanding this background may make understanding my perceptions easier. First, I am a faculty member and have worked in higher education for a total of thirty four years. I spent my first three years at a major urban University, funded by the State of Michigan. When the riots of 1968 erupted in Detroit, I decided that rural living might be preferable and found a position at a small private liberal arts institution in the State of Ohio that offers only undergraduate degrees. I have been on the faculty there ever since. The institution I work for is a very good one in many ways. We have a sabbatical program that allows faculty members to be away on fully paid research leaves every fifth year, and all of our students spend a year and a half in their programs involved in research projects. During the interview process for this position, I asked the Dean if the time I had spent as a faculty member in Detroit would be counted toward tenure and he said with a smile that I should rest assured that all things would be appropriately considered when the time came. Since the College had Christian roots, I believed him. Several years later, I asked the same Dean when I would be considered for tenure and he responded that anyone so concerned about tenuring must have something wrong with him. That response led me to the *American Association of University Professors* to discover the rules which regulated the granting of tenure. In the subsequent years I became more and more involved in faculty issues and in June of this past year I finished a four year period of service as President of that organization.

While I am a biologist, I have been in a unique position to watch and be involved in some of the changes in American Higher Education, especially over the past four years. But it is my discipline that has uniquely helped me understand those changes. As a biologist, I understand the concept of evolution and the forces that can bring about change. There have, indeed, been unique forces at work in American Higher Education and those forces have created significant change in the world I entered in the middle 1960's. Those changes have resulted in a new awareness among faculty, mobilized by what they perceive as threats to the quality of higher education in the States. Recently I received notice by e-mail of a Faculty Association symposium to be held in California whose title is "The Corporate Model for Higher Education – A Faculty Activist Agenda". The announced subject of this meeting is the consideration of practical strategies to advance faculty rights and concerns for higher education in the face of governmental and managerial initiatives to restructure public higher education along the lines of private sector corporations.

Let me go back to the beginning of my term as President of the AAUP in 1992. At that time we were witnessing wide scale attacks on tenure in the

States. Everyone seemed to be in the attack mode. A private foundation called the Pew Foundation was funding initiative to find alternatives to tenure. They sponsored Round Table discussions charged with finding new ways to run academic institutions more efficiently. Unfortunately, faculty members were not asked to be participants in the discussions. Often these panels concluded that tenure was the villain and that unproductive tenured faculty were the causes of lethargy in academia. I was not asked to be a participant in one of these "discussions" until late in my four years as President. When faced with such an assault, it seemed logical to look at the criticisms and to respond to them. So we began an effort to answer the criticisms and to provide data which would speak to the assertions that faculty were unproductive and ineffective.

But when these responses began to be made, the ground shifted and tenure itself seemed no longer to be the issue. A new set of charges began to appear. They involved something called "post-tenure review". The basis for the need for such reviews was the feeling that faculty members are not reviewed after tenure and that as a result, they become unproductive and lazy. Many, it was asserted, lectured from aging notes that were never updated. Another part of the argument for post-tenure review was that faculty members were staying longer and longer in their positions, given the federal government's uncapping of mandatory retirement at the age of 65. This, it was asserted, was creating a profession that was keeping young faculty members out and creating a faculty that was old and increasingly out of touch.

No one, however, seemed to want to see if the basic assumptions were valid. The fact that faculty members were not staying on into old age was not relevant to the argument, nor was the fact that more and more faculty members were retiring early rather than staying on even to the age of 65. And the fact was not thought relevant that young people were being kept out of the profession by decisions made at the highest levels to convert full time tenure track positions to part-time and adjunct positions – positions which could be offered to faculty at much lower salaries and to faculty members who received no health care or retirement benefits. When I did get a chance to answer some of these charges on a Pew Round Table panel, I asked an administrator who was arguing for post-tenure reviews whether he was aware of any such schemes which had identified unproductive faculty. He responded by saying that he knew there were few such faculty members, but that the post-tenure reviews were required to prove to members of governing boards that we were, in fact, productive as faculty members. I, in turn, asked him if our problem was a public relations problem which was needed to help convince trustees that we were productive, why we were being asked to spend huge amounts of money on fruitless post-tenure reviews whose results we already knew? He responded that I sounded just like a faculty member.

In light of the pressures to implement post-tenure reviews, the AAUP developed a statement on post-tenure review which argued that such reviews were not to be vehicles for retenuring a person – or for removing tenure. Our statement appeared just in time to see the ground shift again. The newest wave of attacks on academics takes the form of concerns about governance. The arguments have held that the traditional pattern of university governance which has involved faculty members, administrators and members of governing boards acting as partners was inadequate to the running of a modern university. Faculty input into decision-making causes the processes involved to be too slow and the debates which produce a coherent curriculum prevent the institution from being able to make timely change.

The latest evidence of this change in attitude about the proper role of faculty in academic governance is to be found in the statement issued this year by the *Association of Governing Boards*, an organization that speaks for Trustees of academic institutions nationally. Its major conclusion is that "the needs for greater accountability, the demands of technology, and shifting requirements within the academic job market require a different kind of decision making – one that shared governance, with its deliberate and collegial practices, is no longer capable of rendering". In looking at these trends and trying to make sense of them, it occurred to me that each assault, in turn, was not what it seemed to be. The demands for the elimination of tenure were not really about faculty deadwood and the advocates of post-tenure review understood that there are very few dysfunctional faculty members in our colleges and universities. The real issues have been power and control and the driving force behind all the various proposals for change is economic in nature and grows out of concern for and about the "bottom line" in the balance sheet.

The reality is that over the past ten years, membership on Boards of Trustees of both private and public colleges and universities has been drawn from individuals who have achieved success in the business world. Often these appointments are political and are made by the Governor of the State. In Ohio, for example, the Governor who served in his office for eight years appointed almost the entire membership of the Board of Trustees of the University of Akron, a major State University in Ohio. All of the appointments to the Board have been from his political party (the Republican Party) and have been people who are Chief Executive Officers of Business in the State. While I respect his right to make these appointments, those appointed come with the understandings of the work place that were formed in their businesses. Faculty became employees, not partners. Economies call, in their view, for heavy use of part-time employees rather than full time employees. Management is top down, not democratic. Such views have given rise to the statement we see from the Association of Governing Boards.

Having reached this conclusion, I made the suggestion in the final speech I gave to the AAUP while President that we needed to change our strategy as faculty members in dealing with the changes we are seeing. Rather than focus on responses to questions which were only rhetorical and largely empty, we needed to focus on questions that impacted excellence. If our educational system were seen through this lens, answers to the challenges, I argued, would become clear. I asked if the extensive use of part-time faculty members serves the needs of our students. Now over forty-five percent of all instructions in higher education in the States is delivered by part-time and adjunct faculty. Do faculty who have no offices and are appointed to their assignments the night before a course begins have the support they need to teach our students effectively? Are such faculty best able to answer questions students have if they have to be on another campus teaching – often as many as 10 courses a semester – rather than available to students during non-classroom hours? Does the fact that these individuals have no access to computers or links to the internet interfere with their ability to work as effectively as full time faculty members? Framing the issues in these terms may help American faculty to see where and how the best can be achieved. Only when we examine these issues from the perspective of excellence do we, I believe, end up with the best approach to a challenge.

I would just like to end with a description of a new development facing Higher Education not only in the States but potentially world wide. Providers of Education have appeared that offer their education through distance learning. The Western Governor's University is an on-line University that began offering instruction just this past fall. Fortunately only ten students "enrolled." We have a University in Ohio which offers degrees to students who recruit their own instructors from other Universities. Contracts with these teachers are negotiated by the student, who pays for the instruction, in addition to tuition to the sponsoring institution. I received a call from a student about to earn a degree in this program last week who confessed to me that she should not have been admitted and told me that she could not write. The University of Phoenix is a multibranched amoeba that once accredited, has established branches in at least fifteen states. The faculty (called Faculty Facilitators) of these Universities are all part-time and adjuncts, except for four individuals and the courses are developed by committee. The syllabi for these courses are divided into topics, with the number of minutes to be spent on each topic indicated. Each of these new developments represents an approach to higher education that can best be called "entrepreneurial." The goal of the University of Phoenix is to make money for stockholders. The Western Governor's hope to eliminate the cost of faculty, administrators and buildings. The Ohio effort involves nothing but profit for the admitting institution. But each of these developments needs to be held up to the mirror of excellence. That mirror will magnify the good features and expose the blemishes for all of us to see. That mirror needs to be used by faculty members in all countries of the world.

Teaching vs. Research and (Part-of) Lifetime Faculty at German Universities

Jürgen Kohler

The subject of my comments will be teaching vs. research and part-time adjunct vs. full-time faculty. While sorting out the scope of the topic, I was not quite sure where best to begin. I decided to start at the end, that is with part-time adjunct vs. full-time faculty, and then decided to modify the given topic somewhat more. From my German point of view the problem lies somewhere else and needs to be defined differently. Whereas Americans may consider part-time adjunct vs. full-time faculty a question worth raising, I think in Germany the problem lies with tenured faculty vs. non-tenured faculty. When it comes to discussing staff matters this subject is really at the center of the debate in Germany. To be more precise, the issue concerns the role of what we call *Mittelbau*. A number of participants of the conference documented here have tried to translate this term: Neither "junior lecturer" nor "assistant professor" are adequate translations, for they trigger a set of wrong associations. Since there is really no group in the American academic world equivalent to our "Mittelbau" I shall stick with the term. We can roughly translate it as middle-range university personnel. In terms of status they are at the rank of university assistants, but clearly not members of the professoriat. Members of this group may be tenured civil servants at the rank of *Akademischer Rat*, or *Assistants* with a three to six year contract or *Wissenschaftliche Mitarbeiter* with anywhere from three years to lifetime employment. Thus, I may be permitted to stick to the generic term *Mittelbau*. Concerning the role and function of *Mittelbau* the German university is in a definite position of transition and it is unclear what the future has in store for us. This is why I will subdivide my

Jürgen KOHLER: Former President of Greifswald University (until 2000); he was Professor of Law at the universities of Köln, Konstanz, and Bielefeld, before becoming founding Professor of Civil Law at the newly inaugurated faculty for Jurisprudence and Political Science at the University of Greifswald.

topic into two parts. First I am going to describe what the situation has been for the last decades until now, and second where we may be heading.

At present there is in Germany a relatively small number of life-time academic staff below the professorial level and, as compared for example to the British system, a relatively greater number of professors. All in all, there are three tiers to the system. At the top we find the professors, either chairs (C4) or associate professors (C2/3). The former are fully in control of both research and teaching and have at their side secretarial staff and assistants. The latter, the C2/3 category of professors, are somewhat comparable to Associate Professors in the US, who may or may not enjoy similar privileges. Though there is no difference in their academic rights the two types of professors are categorized by their pay-level, by their access to equipment and staff, and by prestige.

Below that level there is a relatively small tier of what we call "Akademische Räte," or "Lehrkräfte für besondere Aufgaben." It is their job to maintain basic teaching services and take care of administration. There is a number of them in the sciences and also in the humanities; less so in medicine or law or economics departments. There are relatively few of them in total numbers as compared to the entirety of university staff, and they are usually employed for life and work full-time. The third tier in the system, which is quite considerable in numbers, is what we call the "Wissenschaftliche Mitarbeiter" or "Wissenschaftliche Assistenten." Here we have a group that stays at the university for a limited period, usually up to about three to six years (with few exceptions who have unlimited contracts). They are attached to a chair or an institute rendering service in teaching under the auspices of that professor or institute. They also assist in research projects for that professor or at that institute. They are usually given time to work towards their own qualification, be it their dissertation or their habilitation. This third tier is quite large and significant within the German system.

What are the merits and demerits of such a structure, with special regard to the group mentioned last? I am going to list them as pros and cons, but you may well argue that certain aspects which I list as an advantage may well be called a disadvantage, and vice versa. And I myself might, on second thoughts, place a number of pros under cons. It is all a matter of perspective and focus. The first pro is that the integration of teaching and research is restricted to professors; in principle at least. If I were to advance a serious explanation beyond that of status, this focus on professors does ensure the unity of research and learning at a high level – at least in theory. And maybe there is again some element of Humboldt at work in this structure. The system also allows for a close collaboration of assistants with his or her professor. This ensures a certain element of effectiveness in the focus of research of that professor or that institute. Thirdly, and again that may be more a con than a pro, there is a "school-building" effect built into that system, where you gather disciples around you who carry on your message. But it is just this effect, I daresay, that may be a decided disadvantage (when the message is mediocre). Fourthly, these people are at university only for a limited period of time, and a lot of them will not make the pitch for a full-time professorship afterwards. Hence a lot of them leave university after a period of apprenticeship. This means that there is an element of disseminating knowledge by disseminating people. In present-day terminology we are talking about a mode of technology transfer. There is an element of transfer in transferring people who produce knowledge, rather than transferring the product of knowledge. Here we have an aspect of transfer efficiency that must be considered when appreciating the German university staff system. On the other hand, we can say there are a number of cons. There certainly is a marked dependency of assistants on the whim of their professors, which may lead to numbing effect concerning independence of mind and scholarly initiative at an early stage of the career. In many cases it also has a detrimental effect on the selection process for young academic hopefuls. In a number of academic disciplines job opportunities from outside the academy are much more attractive than what the university has to offer, especially for those who welcome the challenges of the open market and would seek greater independence there. Not only the meager income puts people off from entering upon a university career, it is quite likely that many are deterred by having to remain in a subaltern position for too long at universities. This "burn-out" effect is visible in the field of economics and law, medicine, sciences or engineering, i. e. any of those subjects where there is strong competition from industry or the open market.

A third element puts a brake on effectiveness; this is the difficulty to establish a coherent and reliable system of instruction. Due to the current frequent changes in staff, it is very hard to establish anything like a systematic curriculum or canon. Whether this is a good thing or a bad thing needs to be discussed. Again, it seems to be inherent to the German traditional understanding of universities as places where students seek knowledge rather than are taught. This may be the last gasps of the Humboldtian concept of self-governance and academic independence of students, which disappeared with the onset of the overcrowded multiversity a few decades ago. In our current mass universities with student numbers that defy any notion of academic freedom, this hallowed tradition may have to be reconsidered. Coming from a university with a GDR background, I know that it is particularly this point where the West and the East German systems of higher education seem to be on different tracks. A lot of my colleagues who have an East German background greatly lament the loss of a stable tutor system on the middle staff level.

This is the state of affairs at the moment. I am now going to talk about the future as I see it, and as designed in the German University Rectors' Conference papers. As colleague Weiler points out, the Rectors' Conference recently passed a very controversial paper on the re-structuring of the academic staff. Professor Weiler refers to the professorial level and the salary structure which forms only part of that paper. Another section of that paper deals with the qualification process for young academics. German universities follow the double qualification requirement of doctoral dissertation plus post-doctoral habilitation. The latter may be difficult to place within an American background. Somebody once jokingly explained to me what it means: A dissertation is a text which shows that the candidate has comprehended something that was new to him or her; and a habilitation is a text which is designed to make other people understand something new to them. It may however best be compared to the second, significant book after the dissertation which is usually necessary for promotion from assistant to associate professor in the US. By the same token the Habilitation is the membership ticket to professorial status.

In terms of time this system means that people are anywhere between 35 or 45 years old depending on the discipline before they are actually formally recognized as being eligible for a vacant professorship. It seems to be an enormous waste of human resources to bar young academics institutionally from academic independence for so long. So the idea is to lower the profile of the "Habilitation", maybe even to do away with it, and to get assistants involved in independent research and teaching at a much earlier stage. The freshly launched DFG-Emmy-Noether program is designed to achieve just that effect. This development stands in clear contrast to present usage, for it is designed to sever the strong links of dependency which have hitherto been characteristic for the relationship between the professor and his disciples. What effect that change within the concept of qualification will have on the efficiency of research needs to be discussed. But it may encourage more people to expect a challenging future at universities. It may also alert those who lack the talent or qualifications for teaching or who do not have what it takes for a career in research to find other options. To learn this at the age of 30 or 32 is preferable to getting the bad news at 42, the current median age of habilitation. At this time we witness an interesting dual development in the sense that the change in formal recruitment for a professorship goes hand in hand with the re-definition of the role of assistant. I should also mention here that this new concept should have a side effect of recruiting more women into academic careers. One reason why women have played a limited role in academics resides in the obvious problem they face when they try to harmonize their desire for a family with a university career. The dissertation-cum-habilitation qualification takes you near your forties which creates some difficulties for women who want to start a family.

To sum up, we are moving from a certain structure of dependence on the assistant level toward stronger independence; we are moving from a long term career pattern into a short term career pattern. Furthermore, we are trying to open recruitment opportunities to outsiders rather than stick to the staggered career trajectory of personnel development. In addition, the pay structure for professors will be adjusted to have one instead of two types of pay levels. Then competition after attaining professorial tenure will increase, because performance-linked pay is one element of this new policy. My short presentation is supposed to give an idea of the problems on hand. At this point I will not elaborate the issues any further.

I will now return to the first part of our topic, and that is teaching vs. research. I am going to be brief as well. The unity of teaching and research as defined in the traditional German university has lead to the strong role of the professor. He is the only academic agent to unite both elements in his person. Here we should not only talk about the relationship of academic staff levels and the German concept of the "research university" when it comes to discussing teaching vs. research. Instead we should talk about the roles of the institutions that are involved in teaching and research. The real issue to be debated should be the role of the extra-university research institutions vs. the university. Many of us in Germany observe but few explicitly comment on a strong perception in the public view that universities are predominantly places for teaching. Unfortunately, their significance as research institutions is being reduced in the eyes and activities of politicians, too. There are a lot of institutions outside universities that take over more and more research responsibilities, and there is much more focus in politics and public opinion on research institutions outside universities. Whether we consider academies, or Max-Planck, Fraunhofer, Leibniz, etc., and whatever way we look at the research scene, a fact is that the number of institutions outside universities are increasing, and that more and more money is going towards these institutions. At the same time research as one of the key purposes and core functions of the universities is not as strongly emphasized. Research is not in the limelight as it ought to be and used to be. So there has been a long-range shift and seachange in the function of universities in Germany which must be closely scrutinized; I would call it a slow and gradual decline of the research orientation of German universities over the past decades. This decline needs to be considered from an institutional point of view, and we need to ask whether it is sound policy to move on in this direction. As I understand the American experience in the 40s or 50s, when the same question was discussed there, their answer was to reattach research closely to the universities instead of allowing universities and research to drift asunder. We need to reconsider this matter.

To sum up: On the one hand teaching vs. research is a matter of staffing. On the other it is also a matter of institutions. Both sides must be borne in mind. We should stress both aspects in our reform discussion.

MOBILITY AND SERVICE:
THE DUAL ROLE OF HIGHER EDUCATION IN
U.S. SOCIETY

Robert GLIDDEN

Whereas institutions for the liberal education of youth are essential to the
progress of arts and sciences, important to morality, virtue and religion, friendly
to the peace, order and prosperity of society, and honorable to the government
that encourages and patronizes them, be it enacted … [t]hat there shall be an
university instituted and established in the town of Athens – Charter for Ohio
University, adopted 18 February 1804.

Citizens of the United States of America have great respect for their Constitution, which they view as a living document, able to address future concerns
because of its scope, balance, and universal principles. Many of those principles still shape higher education either directly, by influencing charters such as
the one above that established my own institution, or indirectly, by influencing
debate about issues from curriculum to funding. So before I report on the state
of higher education in America, citing statistics and describing our present situation, I would like to comment about the core philosophy of an immigrant
nation with a dual character of mobility and service. Just as our Constitution
balances the branches of government – Executive, Legislative, and Judicial –
so, too, do our universal values of prosperity and civic virtue balance the missions of our learning institutions.

The United States is often called a "melting pot," a land of opportunity, a
place where one can get ahead and elevate his or her station in life by industri-
ousness and creativity. This is called the American dream, the American ideal.

Robert GLIDDEN: President of Ohio University, Chairman of the American Council on Education Commission on Leadership and Institutional Effectiveness, Chairman of the Board of
Directors for the Ohio Aerospace Institute; former appointments at Florida State University,
at Wright State University, Ohio, at the University of Oklahoma, and as Executive Director
of the National Association of Schools of Music and National Association of Schools of Art
and Design in Washington, DC. His interest in national higher education affairs in the U.S.
is particularly strong in matters of accreditation, educational assessment, and arts policy.

In many respects higher education has been the embodiment of the American ideal, particularly as the means by which people can enhance their quality of life. Historically, to the current day, the great majority of each American generation has exceeded the standard of living of their parents, primarily because of our educational system.

However, there is another less-discussed aspect of the American ideal that ensures prosperity for future generations. This is the service aspect, which we would consider part of civic virtue and which reminds each citizen to give back to the society that created the American dream and the personal opportunity. One can see that dual influence even in our own charter, which discusses progress, not in opportunistic tones but in virtuous ones: "friendly to the peace, order and prosperity of society."

Let us look deeper into these concepts. Mobility, historically, had to do with class structure – a kind of linear birthright that usually assured privileges to the elite and burdens to the disenfranchised. In truth, most of our earliest institutions, such as Harvard and Yale, primarily trained clergy to maintain English cultural norms and provide a new land with an educated elite. [1] Whatever the motive, the fact that our early institutions trained clergy led, inescapably, to the infusion of morality into our educational system, and that helped create the service aspect ensuring balance and, eventually, access to greater numbers of citizens and residents. As scholar and author Lawrence A. Cremin notes in *American Education: The National Experience*:

> The republican style in American education was compounded of four fundamental beliefs: that education was crucial to the vitality of the Republic; that a proper republican education consisted of the diffusion of knowledge; the nurturance of virtue (including patriotic civility), and the cultivation of learning; that schools and colleges were the best agencies for providing a proper republican education on the scale required. ... The very novelty of the idea bespoke a variety of approaches, and indeed one leading theme in the history of American education during the first century of the Republic is the remarkable multiplicity of institutional ways and means by which states and localities moved to the creation of public school systems. [2]

---

[1]   See the online essay "Evolution of Learning Assistance in Higher Education," by Martha Casazza, who writes: "The primary mission of early colleges such as Harvard and Yale was to train clergy and to preserve and maintain the cultural norms that were brought from Europe. The goal was to provide an educated elite who could lead the new society" <http://nlu.nl.edu/ace/Resources/Documents/LearningAsst.html>

[2]   Lawrence A. Cremin, *American Education: The National Experience, 1783–1876* (New York: Harper & Row, 1980) 48.

Because of that "remarkable multiplicity," class structure began to change in America and that change in an upward direction is what we call "mobility." Social mobility, of course, is now defined by opportunity – the success of one entrepreneur, sometimes at the expense of another. Service, on the other hand, is defined by civic virtue, concern for the "other" who otherwise pays the expense. Higher education in America has dealt slowly but effectively with that paradox, recognizing the hardships of competition, especially in an immigrant nation that continually raises the level of competitiveness by welcoming the best and brightest to our shores. Moreover, mobility is concerned about know-how and skill, and we might define these as opportunity's tools. Know-how and skill lead to the inevitable emphasis on applied as well as philosophical learning in U.S. institutions. Schools and colleges began to recognize this as early as 1862 with the signing by President Lincoln of the Morrill Act, providing lands and funds for schools that taught agricultural and mechanical techniques. This act, and a sister act providing for more schools and greater access in 1890, re-emphasized opportunity's tools – know-how and skill – as ever more streams of immigrants came to America in search of their individual dreams. Educators knew that those with the best tools are usually the most effective or successful in society. Service, however, was concerned, then as now, about the use and distribution of that know-how and skill.

Of course, the American ideal *is* an ideal requiring access for all. Access has been the topic of debate since the inception of the United States. While it has been a principle of American democracy that every citizen has a right to the highest level of education for which he or she has the intellectual capacity, our own history illustrates a reluctance to share that ideal freely with others. This, too, defines the importance of that dual role of mobility and service. Without a service commitment to society, America might never have transcended its exclusionary past. As Lawrence Cremin writes, "Rich or poor, German and French, Protestant and Catholic – but not black and red. ... Blacks and [American] Indians were excluded from citizenship and hence from education for self- government."[3] To this day, access for minorities is an issue of concern, even at Ohio University, one of the oldest in America and one of the first to graduate an African-American, John Newton Templeton, in 1828.

Without education's influence, Amendments 15 and 19 to the U.S. Constitution – assuring voting privileges to all men, regardless of race, in 1870, and to all women in 1920 – may not have been achieved, however belatedly. Higher education, in particular, had an important influence and impact on the status

---

[3] Cremin 7.

of women in American society. Because of equal access to higher education, women have advanced to positions of prominence and leadership in business and the professions, thanks, in large part, to pioneering women like Catharine E. Beecher, who established female seminaries in the East and Midwest between the years 1823 and 1832. Catharine's legacy is not as widely known as her famous author sister and abolitionist, Harriet Beecher Stowe; but she was equally as influential with regard to the education of women, again looking to civic virtue and service as the keys to unlock equal opportunity for women seeking knowledge and know-how. Consider this passage:

> Let the women of a country be made virtuous and intelligent, and the men will certainly be the same ... If this be so, as none will deny, then to American women, more than to any others on earth, is committed the exalted privilege of extending over the world those blessed influences that are to renovate degraded men, and "clothe all climes with beauty." [4]

Again, through the establishment of her female seminaries as well as through her writings about civic virtue, Beecher pioneered access to education for women as an aspect of service to society. Thus, access for all to higher educational opportunities has been an important issue throughout the history of the United States, through the Morrill Acts of 1862 and 1890 and continuing especially since the end of World War II and the advent of the GI Bill. The latter granted funds to thousands of returning veterans to study at institutions of higher learning. These veterans, many of whom were in their teens when they were called to military service, had no real training or job experience other than military skills and faced little prospect of securing increasingly technical jobs in industry or leadership positions in business. Many of them, of course, looked to higher education to ensure mobility – a better way of life – in a time of peace and anticipated prosperity. Without the GI Bill, those veterans could have returned without jobs or prospects to an America whose values they helped preserve, but whose opportunities had passed them by. Instead, they went to school. And that, probably, is the single greatest turning point in the history of higher education in the United States, particularly with regard to access. It changed the way America thought about higher education because,

---

[4]   Catharine E. Beecher, *A Treatise on Domestic Economy, for the Use of Young Ladies at Home, and at School* (Boston: Marsh, Capen, Lyon, and Webb, 1841) 9, 13, as cited and discussed by Cremin in *American Education: The National Experience.* See also Beecher's *Educational Reminiscences and Suggestions* (New York: JB Ford and Co., 1874), in which the author states: "We are constantly meeting in newspapers statements of liberal benefactions from women to endow colleges and professional schools for men; is it unreasonable to hope that the time is near when unmarried women and widows will find equal privileges" (p. 265).

when those veterans graduated and began careers, they not only achieved a measure of the American dream, they passed that ideal on to their families as a key factor of upward mobility. However, let it also be said that without America's service commitment – which created the educational opportunity for veterans in the first place – we could have risked another Great Depression instead of the 1950s economic boom.

In ensuing decades, ever more numbers of people sought degrees. Technology had been important since the passage of the Morrill Acts and the industrialization eras of the 1920s and '50s; but the space race of the 1960s also influenced education in America. The space race led to programs for advanced education, particularly in science, but also to the creation of specialized, technical, and community colleges to serve applicants with more diverse goals in a variety of programs. This in turn fed the continuing demand for greater levels of access. According to educators Arthur M. Cohen and Florence B. Brawer:

> Community colleges have effected notable changes in American education, especially by expanding access. Well into the middle of the twentieth century, higher education had elements of mystery within it. Only one young person in seven went to college, and most students were from the middle and upper classes. To the public at large, which really had little idea of what went on behind the walls, higher education was a clandestine process, steeped in ritual. The demystification of higher education, occasioned by the democratization of access, has taken place steadily. Given marked impetus after World War II by the GI Bill, when the first large scale financial aid packages were made available and people could be reimbursed not only for their tuition but also for their living expenses while attending college, college going increased rapidly, so that by the 1970s three in every eight persons attended [5]

Because it is recognized as an "engine of mobility" by the society and is therefore highly sought after, American higher education functions very much in a market economy. Institutions compete with others, particularly in the same sector of higher education but also across sectors, for students, for resources, and for favorable image with the public and with decision makers. Because of such competition, universities in the U.S. function much more like businesses in many of their attitudes than the typical European university. American universities, in order to compete successfully for students, have a tendency to give students what they want, not only in the types of credentials and courses offered but also in the specific content of courses. American higher education, then, tends to be more practice-oriented in many of its offerings than its Eu-

---

5   Arthur M. Cohen and Florence B. Brawer, *The American Community College* (San Francisco: Jossey-Bass, 1982) 19.

ropean counterparts. Ironically, however, such competitiveness has reminded us about the importance of our service role, especially when seeking financial support from the federal government and state legislatures.

In a telling essay discussing insufficient funding of state education, author John J. Clayton writes:

> When I was a child, living in an apartment in New York City, a refugee named Theodore would come every few months to wash our windows. I remember his buckets and the black leather straps he hooked onto the stone ledge, seven floors above an alley. I remember his thick Polish accent, his rimless glasses, his severity. He seemed to have weathered into leather himself. Paid by the window, he worked with amazing speed. One afternoon my mother called me in to watch him at work.
>
> "You see that man? What do you think he's doing?"
>
> "Washing windows," I suggested.
>
> "Let me tell you what he's really doing: That man is putting two sons and a daughter through university! You understand? And that's America." [6]

Clayton, an English professor at the University of Massachusetts-Amherst, has said this story made America "seem heroic – a land of possibilities, of social mobility through education provided by the people." It has become the responsibility, not only of professors but primarily of university presidents like myself, to remind government about its own principles and the dual nature of mobility and service, without which the American educational system would not be the global model in terms of student access, program diversity and institutional variety, from community college to post-doctoral research institution. Perhaps this concept is best expressed by Philip E. Austin, President of the University of Connecticut, who writes:

> [A]ll the great public universities across the United States [share] a common tradition and a common set of assumptions about America's future.
>
> That tradition – and those assumptions – embody three concepts that are as valid as they are familiar to people concerned with higher education. ... They define our future agenda.
>
> The first is excellence in our academic programs – at the undergraduate, graduate, and professional levels, in the classrooms, the laboratories, and the libraries.
>
> The second is access for the people of [their state], regardless of race, gender, national origin – or economic condition.
>
> The third is service – to the state and beyond. [7]

---

[6] John J. Clayton, "America is Destroying Public Higher Education," *Chronicle of Higher Education* 29 January 1992: A48.

[7] As appears in Philip E. Austin's inaugural address, given 17 April 1997, at Jorgensen Auditorium, University of Connecticut.

Again note the emphasis on excellence, access and service. That is what all great colleges and universities, including my own Ohio University, strive for in partnerships and programming. The dual model of higher education in America has a long history and continues to evolve and develop. Because of its adaptability, our institutions have been able to weather the changes and meet the challenges that each era brings.

Let me now turn to those issues forming my specific topic, namely student issues. Much of my commentary thus far has addressed access to higher education in America, an important student concern, to be sure. I will expand on that by talking about the scope and diversity of the higher education enterprise in the United States, say a few words about types of degrees offered and student retention and completion, and then conclude with comments about the cost of higher education as a socio-political issue.

Access and Participation

Factors that enhance access to higher education for the people of the United States include the broad scope and great diversity of our learning institutions. In its survey of 1997 the National Center for Educational Statistics reports a total of 6,689 postsecondary educational institutions. [8] Of that number, 1,868 are institutions that offer only programs of less-than-two years' duration, and 2,434 are two-year institutions. Most of these schools offer technical courses of study and most of the two-year public institutions are community colleges that also offer the Associate of Arts or Associate of Science degrees. That leaves, in the four-year college and university sector, 2,387 institutions. Of that number, 634 are public, 1,588 are private, non-profit, and 165 are private, for-profit.

---

[8]   See National Center for Educational Statistics <http://nces.ed.gov/Ipeds/c9697/C97Rate.HTML>

Types of Postsecondary Institutions in U.S., 1997

Public, 4-year	634
Private, nonprofit, 4-year	1,588
Private, for-profit, 4-year	165
Public, 2-year	1,223
Private, nonprofit, 2-year	369
Private, for-profit, 2-year	842
Public, less-than-2-year	223
Private, nonprofit, less-than-2-year	98
Private, for-profit, less-than-2-year	1,587
Total	*6,689*

It is obvious from these data that U.S. students have many choices. Even among institutions in the college and university category, the community in which we are most interested here, there are many options. *U.S. News and World Report*'s 1999 rankings of "best colleges" includes 1,400 four-year institutions (*i.e.,* institutions that offer at least the baccalaureate degree), categorized into four tiers: national universities, national liberal arts colleges, regional universities, and regional liberal arts colleges, as well as some unclassified, special-purpose institutions. [9] For my own state of Ohio, with a population of 11 million, there are 61 colleges and universities listed. Twelve are "national universities," eight are "national liberal arts colleges," eleven are "regional universities," 23 are "regional liberal arts colleges," and seven are special-purpose institutions (schools of art, music, business, etc.). All of these institutions grant baccalaureate degrees; some grant associate degrees as well. Twenty-five offer the master's as the highest degree, and 18 offer the doctorate. [10] Thirteen of the 61 are state-supported or state-assisted universities.

Another way of describing colleges and universities in the U.S. is the classification by the Carnegie Foundation for the Advancement of Teaching. Carnegie sorts institutions into ten categories: two each for Research, Doctoral Degree-Granting, Master's Comprehensive, and Baccalaureate, one category for Associate-Degree-Granting, and one for Specialized (usually single-purpose) institutions. The differences among these categories are size and scope. Research I universities are more focused on research and attract more

---

[9]   *U.S. News and World Report:* "America's Best Colleges" (Washington, DC, 1998) 114.

[10]   *U.S. News and World Report* 224-231.

federal research funds than Research II universities, for example. Research II universities grant more doctoral degrees in more disciplines than Doctoral institutions. Baccalaureate I colleges grant more than 40% of their degrees in the liberal arts disciplines, and Baccalaureate II colleges focus more on specialized fields. Using Ohio once again as an example of the diversity of institutions in just one state, we have the following array of collegiate institutions according to the Carnegie classification: [11]

Higher Education Institutions in Ohio, by Carnegie Classification

Research I	3
Research II	2
Doctoral I	5
Doctoral II	2
Master's (Comprehensive) I Colleges and Universities	8
Master's (Comprehensive) II Colleges and Universities	3
Baccalaureate I Colleges	8
Baccalaureate II Colleges (including branch campuses)	27
Associate of Arts Colleges	15
Specialized Institutions	25

Thus, U.S. students can choose from a very broad selection of colleges and universities, even within one state of the United States.

Who goes to college in the U.S.? Increasing numbers and percentages of Americans are realizing that we have entered an information age, never to turn back; thus, students are taking advantage of opportunities for post-secondary education to prepare themselves for a world that may be unforgiving for those with only secondary school education. The increase in postsecondary enrollment from 1985 to 1995 was more than 16% (12.247 million to 14.262 million), and the increase is projected to be another 9% from 1995 to 2005 (to 15.516 million). The percentage of women among the postsecondary population has increased from 52% in 1985 to 55% in 1995, and it is projected to increase further, to 57%, by the year 2005. The percentage of students who study full-time has remained the same at approximately 58% and that percentage is projected to remain the same through 2005.

---

[11]   See Carnegie Foundation <http://www.carnegiefoundation.org/cihe/>.

Enrollment Statistics – All U.S. Postsecondary Institutions (in thousands)[12]

Year	Total	Sex		Attendance Status		Control	
		Men	Women	Full-Time	Part-Time	Public	Private
1985	12,247	5,818	6,429	7,075	5,172	9,479	2,768
1995	14,262	6,343	7,919	8,129	6,133	11,092	3,140
2005*	15,516	6,684	8,833	9,085	6,432	12,101	3,415

*projected

In four-year institutions – the colleges and universities – percentages of women are comparable. The percentage of women attending college increased from 50% to 54% from 1985 to 1995, and it is projected to increase to over 56% by 2005. The percentage of students attending four-year colleges or universities full-time appears to be stable through the years but it is somewhat higher than those engaged in all of postsecondary education. Nearly 70% of the four-year college/university attendees studied full-time in 1985; that number increased to slightly over 70% in 1995 and it is projected to be 71% in 2005. The percentage of students attending public colleges and universities is stable through the years at 67%.

Enrollment Statistics – Four-Year Institutions (in thousands)[13]

Year	Total	Sex		Attendance Status		Control	
		Men	Women	Full-Time	Part-Time	Public	Private
1985	7,716	3,816	3,900	5,385	2,331	5,210	2,506
1995	8,769	4,014	4,755	6,152	2,617	5,815	2,955
2005*	9,578	4,205	5,373	6,804	2,774	6,413	3,165

*projected

Despite billions of dollars of student financial aid provided by the federal and state governments in the U.S. to assist lower income families, college participation correlates closely with family income. College participation depends on secondary school completion, of course, and students from low income families graduate from high school at a considerably lesser rate than those from higher income ranges. And whether for financial reasons, family educational values, or both, the following table shows that there is a vast difference between higher and lower income families in the likelihood of success in college (as defined by completion of the baccalaureate degree). These data are from

---

[12] See National Center for Educational Statistics <http://nces.ed.gov/pubs98/pj2008/p98t03.html>.

[13] See National Center for Educational Statistics <http://nces.ed.gov/pubs98/pj2008/p98t04.html>.

1996 and they show that only 5.4% of the unmarried 18 – 24 year-olds in the lowest income group are projected to complete the bachelor's degree, whereas 74% of those from the highest income category graduate will attain the bachelor's degree.

Educational Success by Family Income Level, Unmarried 18 – 24-Year-Olds, 1996 [14]

Income Category	Family Income	H.S. Grad Rate	College Participation	College Completion**
Top Quartile	$71,801	93.4%	79.7%	74.0%
3rd Quartile	$45,035*	87.9%	65.9%	22.6%
2nd Quartile	$45,035*	81.7%	53.9%	15.1%
Lowest Quartile	$24,589	64.9%	34.9%	5.4%

*This figure is the dividing point between the 2nd and 3rd income quartiles.
** Projected completion of the bachelor's degree

   Of serious sociological concern in the U.S. are the participation, retention and degree of success in college by the African-American population. The latest longitudinal data available for college completion rates are from the high school class of 1982. They are compared with the class of ten years previous, 1972. These data show the 37% increase from 1972 to 1982, referred to previously, in the number of students entering post-secondary education (of all types, presumably) and earning at least 10 credits. The baccalaureate completion rate for all students declined from 48.3% to 44.5% during that period, but that decrease is considered modest compared with the much greater percentage of the population who participated in 1982. In that study, however, one notices that the percentage of African-Americans increased rather significantly, from 8.1% of the sample in 1972 to 11.0% in 1982. However, African-Americans' success rate, *i.e.*, completion of the bachelor's degree, dropped from 35.3% to 24.8%, an indication that U.S. institutions still have work to do to achieve diversity and to serve all populations well. Hispanic populations fared better. They increased from 3.5% to 6.4% as a proportion of the total sample, and they also increased their bachelor's degree completion rate from 25.2% to 26.4%. Incidentally, the mean time to degree increased from 1972 to 1982, from 4.5 years in '72 to 4.8 years in '82. Approximately one in eight of the B.A. earners in 1982 required 6.5 years or more to make that accomplishment. [15]

---

[14]   Thomas G. Mortenson, *Postsecondary Education Opportunity 75* (September 1998): 1 – 7.
[15]   Data prepared by Jacqueline King. See The College Board
   <http://www.collegeboard.org/policy/html/trnscr.html>.

Bachelor's Degree Completion Rates by Gender and Race/Ethnicity [16]

	High School Class	BA Completion Rate	% of Sample
Men	1972	50.4	51.2
	1982	46.1	46.2
Women	1972	46.1	48.8
	1982	43.3	53.8
White	1972	50.4	87.2
	1982	48.5	80.1
Black	1972	35.3	8.1
	1982	24.8	11.0
Hispanic	1972	25.2	3.5
	1982	26.4	6.4
Asian	1972	61.9	1.2
	1982	59.2	1.9

Another, more recent set of data from the National Center for Education Statistics shows persistence and rates of attainment of undergraduate degrees. These data are from 1994 and they treat students who were first-time-in-college in 1989. In that five-year period, 25.8% had completed a baccalaureate degree, another 24.1% had attained an Associate of Arts degree or certificate, and 13.3% were still enrolled although they had not yet earned a credential. Also, 36.8% were "drop-outs," *i.e.*, they were no longer enrolled and had not completed a degree or certificate. Of the drop-outs, 48% had first attended a two-year institution and 35.5% had first attended a less-than-two-year school. Of the 49.9% who had attained a degree (B.A. or A.A.) or certificate, most (74%) had attended only one institution and most (79%) had enrolled continuously.

---

[16]   U.S. Department of Education, *The New College Course Map and Transcript Files*. Data are from student academic transcripts collected in longitudinal studies of the high school classes of 1972 and 1982.

Undergraduate Degree Attainment of 1989 First-Time Students by Spring 1994 [17]

	Attained BA	Attained AA or Cert.	No degree, still enrolled	No degree, not enrolled
Total	25.8%	24.1%	13.3%	36.8%
Four-Year	53.3	7.1	15.2	24.4
Two-Year	6.1	32.4	13.6	48.0
Less than Two-Year	0.9	61.1	2.5	35.5

Degree and Enrollment Status of 1989 First-Time Students by Spring 1994 [18]

Attained Degree		49.9%
	Attended one institution	36.9
	Attended more than one institution	13.0
	Enrolled continuously	39.6
	Did not enroll continuously	10.3
Enrolled		13.3%
	One institution	6.4
	Attended more than one institution	6.9
	Enrolled continuously	6.0
	Did not enroll continuously	7.3
Not Enrolled/No Degree		36.8%
	Attended one institution	27.9
	Attended more than one institution	8.9
	Enrolled continuously	25.0
	Did not enroll continuously	11.8

According to data from the U.S. Department of Education's *Digest of Education Statistics 1997,* participation rates for postsecondary education in the United States are somewhat higher than for European nations, particularly in the 18-to-21-year-old age group. [19] Their source was the Organization for Eco-

---

[17] National Center for Education Statistics Beginning Postsecondary Students Study, reported by Jacqueline King <http://www.collegeboard.org/policy/html/degree.html>.

[18] Ibid.

[19] See National Center for Educational Statistics <http://nces.ed.gov/pubs/digest97/d97t390.html>.

nomic Cooperation and Development, and it is somewhat difficult to determine whether the comparisons are accurate. U.S. data are for "higher education" institutions only, but it is not clear what types of institutions in European countries are included. For the 22-25-year-olds and 26-29-year-olds, the percentages of participation are comparable.

Percentage of Population Enrolled in Higher Education [20]

	Age 18 – 21			Age 22 – 25			Age 26 – 29		
	1985	1990	1994	1985	1990	1994	1985	1990	1994
Denmark	7.4	7.4	9.1	16.3	17.9	22.1	8.2	9.3	10.9
Finland	9.3	13.6	16.6	17.3	20.7	27.3	7.9	10.2	12.2
France	19.4	24.6	33.2	10.0	11.8	17.0	4.3	3.9	4.6
Germany*	8.8	8.5	11.2	15.5	15.9	17.2	8.9	10.4	10.3
Netherlands	14.4	17.9	22.1	11.9	13.4	18.4	5.7	4.7	6.2
Norway	8.8	14.4	17.1	13.2	18.9	23.6	5.7	4.7	6.2
Sweden	7.9	8.7	12.3	11.3	11.4	15.3	6.6	6.1	7.2
Switzerland	5.7	6.4	7.6	10.6	12.1	14.2	5.2	6.4	7.1
United States	33.0	36.2	34.9	14.5	17.1	20.9	8.2	8.5	10.4

*Data for 1985 are for former West Germany
Note: Some increases in enrollment rates may be due to more complete reporting by countries.
Source: Organization for Economic Cooperation and Development, Education at a Glance, 1996; and unpublished data.

A significant percentage of bachelor's degree recipients in the United States continue to pursue higher education after completing their first degree. Of those who completed their baccalaureates in 1992 – 93, 27.3% have been enrolled in further study. Those who graduated from professional fields such as engineering, business and management, the health professions, education, public affairs and social services – fields in which there is greater likelihood of employment with only the bachelor's degree – continued at a 23.5% rate. Graduates from the arts and sciences fields (biological sciences, mathematics and other sciences, psychology, social sciences, history and the humanities) continued at a 34.5% rate. [21] The latter are disciplines in which further study is usually required for employment, or they are disciplines that serve as preparation for study in a professional field. Of those 1992 – 93 graduates who enrolled full-time for study beyond the bachelor's degree, 29.5% reported that their aspirations were to earn a doctoral degree and 34.8% were in pursuit of a first professional degree (law, medicine, etc.) [22]

---

[20] Ibid.
[21] See National Center for Educational Statistics <http://nces.ed.gov/pubs/digest97/d97t385.html>.
[22] Ibid.

Types of Degrees and Time to Attainment

In the most recent year for which data are available, 1994–95, U.S. colleges and universities granted 2,141,900 degrees, associate through doctorate. Of that number 25% (539,691) were associate degrees, 54% (1,160,134) were baccalaureates, 19% (397,629) were master's, and 2% (44,446) were doctorates (the Ph.D., Ed.D., etc.). [23]

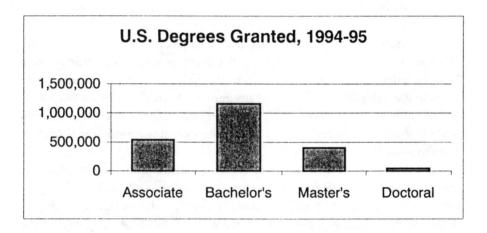

The Associate of Arts degree is typically earned in two years and comprises largely general studies or what is sometimes referred to as liberal education. It is often offered in community colleges as a transfer component to a baccalaureate-degree-granting institution, and in such cases typically constitutes the general studies portion of the baccalaureate degree, other studies at the senior institution being taken in the major discipline. Associate of Arts degrees are also offered by some baccalaureate-degree-granting colleges or universities for students who complete their general studies but elect not to continue toward baccalaureate completion.

Associate of Science degrees are more typically terminal degrees for technical fields and do not transfer readily to colleges and universities. Courses may be transferred one by one, according to their appropriateness to the subsequent course of study, but many senior institutions will not accept the A.S. degree as a unit transfer.

---

[23]   See National Center for Educational Statistics <http://nces.ed.gov/pubs/digest97/d97t253.htm

The baccalaureate degree is the normal "first degree" in the U.S. It is typically four years of study, or in some disciplines such as engineering, five years. It is considered the first professional degree in some fields – *e.g.,* engineering, fine arts, education, business, journalism – but it is also a preparatory degree for professional fields such as law, medicine, or veterinary medicine. Although the bachelor's degree was intended to be a four-year degree, five years are required in many instances. This is partly due to the expanding knowledge base in every discipline and consequent additions to curricula, including external internships; but it is also due to the desire of students – even those enrolled full-time – who may wish to work part-time while pursuing their degrees.

The master's degree is a terminal degree in practice-oriented fields where there is no doctorate, or where the doctorate is considered strictly as a "scholar's degree." Social work and some disciplines within the fine arts would fall into this category. In many other disciplines, particularly the traditional areas of study in the sciences and humanities, the master's degree is taken en route to the doctorate, and in some such disciplines it is passed over altogether and the student focuses on the doctorate itself.

The doctoral degree in American higher education is divided into two categories, and these categories become less well defined with each passing year. One category is the traditional, scholarly doctorate – the Ph.D. degree. Such a degree usually requires a minimum of three years' full-time study beyond the baccalaureate and often more. It always includes a dissertation, which in American academic parlance implies original research. The candidate for the Ph.D. is expected to make a contribution of new knowledge with his/her research or dissertation, and that portion of the course of study is typically one-third to one-half of the effort toward degree completion.

The practice-oriented doctorate, *e.g.,* the Doctor of Education, Doctor of Science, Doctor of Musical Arts, Doctor of Business Administration, was conceived to be of less scholarly orientation but of equal academic effort to the Ph.D. The course of study for these degrees generally comprises more coursework and less independent study than the Ph.D., and the research document is expected to exhibit scholarship but not necessarily original research. Some practice-oriented doctorates require a series of research projects rather than one major project. Practice-oriented doctorates expanded during the 1960s in the U.S., when teachers for colleges and universities were in short supply because of the rapidly increasing undergraduate enrollments during that time. Many of these degrees were designed to develop college and university professors who were more practice- and teaching-oriented than their Ph.D.-holding peers. My personal observation is that there has been less expansion of this type of degree in the U.S. in recent years.

Student Life

The following chart shows characteristics of undergraduate students in the U.S. This information is from 1992–93 but there is no reason to believe that current demographic data would be significantly different from this. More than 55% of America's undergraduate students are female and most students are 23 years of age or younger. It is worthy of note, however, that more than one-fourth are age 30 or older. Whites still make up the great majority of the student population, and 45% of all these students are enrolled in two-year institutions. Nearly 43% list the bachelor's degree as their educational goal. Although 39% indicate that their immediate goal is an associate degree, it should be acknowledged that some of that group may later decide to continue their education in pursuit of the baccalaureate or even a higher degree. Nearly half indicate that they are dependents, *i.e.,* relying on parents or perhaps a spouse for financial support. About one-third are full-time, full-year students, but interestingly only a small percentage, 12.8%, are in residence on a campus. (That might be considered interesting because the stereotype of the "college student" in the U.S. is a full-time student on a residential campus such as my own. In fact, nearly 60% of American students live off campus and nearly 30% live with parents or relatives.)

Characteristics of Undergraduate Students [24]
Percentage Distribution of Undergraduate Students by Selected Characteristics, 1992 – 93

Gender	Male	44.5
	Female	55.5
Age	23 or Younger	55.1
	24 to 29	17.1
	30 or Older	27.8
Race	American Indian/Alaskan Native	1.0
	Asian/Pacific Islander	4.0
	Black, Non-Hispanic	10.3
	Hispanic	8.0
	White, Non-Hispanic	76.8
Institution Type	Public, 2 Year or Less	45.3
	Public, 4 Year Non-Doctoral	13.2
	Public, 4 Year Doctoral	17.9
	Private, Non-Profit, 4 Year or Less, Non-Doctoral	10.0
	Private, Non-Profit, 4 Year Doctoral	5.9
	Private, For-Profit	7.7
Degree Program	Vocational Certificate or Other Undergraduate	18.3
	Associate´s Degree	39.0
	Bachelor´s Degree	42.7
Dependency Status	Dependent	47.9
	Independent Without Dependents	20.5
	Independent With Dependents	31.6
Attendance Pattern	Full-Time, Full-Year	32.8
	Full-Time, Part-Year	13.4
	Part-Time, Full-Year	25.6
	Part-Time, Part-Year	28.1
Residence	On Campus	12.8
	Off Campus	58.8
	With Parents/Relatives	28.3

We often refer to American campuses as "residential" or "commuter," the differences being obvious by those labels, and there are some rather significant differences in the college or university experience according to the residential nature of the campus. My own university has a residential main campus with a

---

[24] See The College Board <http://www.collegeboard.org/policy/html/studch.html>, prepared by Jacqueline King. Source: National Postsecondary Student Aid Study: 1993

population of nearly 20,000 students, 7,000 of whom live on campus in university housing, the remainder living in close proximity because our town is small. (Ohio University also has five regional university centers that enroll 8,000 students; each of these centers is a commuter campus.) Because of the residential environment of our Athens campus we offer many services and opportunities to our students. The university sponsors some 350 student organizations – everything from canoeing and skydiving clubs to a gay and lesbian society and political organizations of every stripe and type. Our residence halls have their own internal community activities and organizations, from radio stations to pizza clubs, and because we require that first- and second- year undergraduate students live in university residence halls, the Residence Life program assumes much responsibility for helping students acclimate to campus life. We have numerous student organizations and honor societies associated with various disciplinary studies; some are professionally oriented, others are service-oriented, and still others are strictly social. But all of these organizations give students outlets for their creative energies and provide them opportunities to learn leadership and teamwork.

We believe it important in a residential campus environment such as ours, one populated largely by 18 – 22-year-old undergraduates, to provide what we would call "values education." We have developed ways to make our students conscious of ethical and responsible behavior in dealing with such problems as high-risk drinking and hate speech. I will not elaborate on that here, but I would invite readers to visit our web site [25] to observe some of our materials and programs.

Cost and Financial Aid

Throughout its history, at least part of the cost of higher education in the United States has been borne by the student and his/her family. The original colleges and universities in our nation were private, of course, and for many Americans, particularly in the east and northeast regions, privately supported education is considered superior and more desirable. It is, of course, more expensive, although various federal and state student financial aid programs have helped to mitigate the cost of private college education substantially. Even though there are many more private colleges and universities, the great majority of Americans attend publicly supported institutions, presumably because of cost and, in many cases, convenience of access.

---

[25]   See <http://www.ohiou.edu/ president/PATH.html>.

The cost of college is a "hot topic" in the U.S. at present. Much of this has been brought about by the great amount of press attention to the cost of high-profile, "brand-name" institutions whose annual cost of attendance often exceeds $30,000 per year. There have been studies of Americans' perception of college costs, and it has been found that most of our citizens believe the cost of public higher education to be more than double what it actually is. The U.S. Congress even appointed a National Commission on the Cost of Higher Education, which some interpreted as a threat by the Congress to intervene with federal legislation to establish price controls on college tuition. In fact, college costs have increased in the U.S. in recent years. In current dollars, *i.e.,* not adjusted for inflation, between 1985–86 and 1995–96 the total cost of attendance at four-year public colleges and universities increased by 77% and the cost increase at private colleges was 91%. Those are the numbers that Americans and the U.S. press find so alarming. However, in *constant* dollars, adjusted for inflation, the increase for public colleges and universities over that ten-year period was a less dramatic 24%, and for private institutions it was 34%.

Ten-Year Changes in Cost of Attendance at Four-Year Colleges and Universities (in Current and Constant 1995 Dollars) [26]

	Public Four Year		Private Four Year	
	Current Dollars	1995 Dollars	Current Dollars	1995 Dollars
1985–86	$3,859	$5,406	$9,228	$12,928
1986–87	4,138	5,669	10,039	13,753
1987–88	4,403	5,794	10,659	14,027
1988–89	4,678	5,885	11,474	14,434
1989–90	4,975	5,970	12,284	14,741
1990–91	5,243	5,961	13,237	15,050
1991–92	5,695	6,276	14,273	15,729
1992–93	6,020	6,436	15,009	16,045
1993–94	6,365	6,632	15,904	16,572
1994–95	6,674	6,761	16,645	16,861
1995–96	6,823	6,707	17,631	17,331
10 Year Increase	77%	24%	91%	34%

Note: Cost of attendance includes tuition, fees, and on campus room and board charges.

---

[26] *Straight Talk About College Costs: Report of the National Commission on the Cost of Higher Education* (Phoenix, AZ: Oryx Press, 1998). See <http://chronicle.com/data/focus.dir/data.dir/0121.98/costreport.htm> for online version of the report.

Now the American Council on Education has launched a "College is Possible" campaign, [27] in which many of us are engaged, to convince Americans that, indeed, costs are reasonable enough and there is sufficient financial assistance available for any citizen to take advantage of higher education opportunities. Not all will be admitted by the elite institutions, of course, but *somewhere*, there is a college opportunity that fits any American who has adequate learning capacity to benefit from higher education.

Of the approximately 16.7 million students presently enrolled in postsecondary study in the United States more than half receive some form of financial aid. Some $60 billion in financial aid was provided to students in 1997 – 98, including federal and nonfederal loans, federal and state grants, and institutional grants. A good, concise source for information about the various grant and loan programs sponsored by the U.S. Government is the College is Possible website. [28] As the name of the site suggests, the emphasis even here is on access and mobility.

Public Versus Private Good

The mobility-service dual model of higher education in America continues to evolve and develop. However, because of funding concerns compounded by increased demand for access – along with other social changes associated with mobility – the current debate in the United States concerns whether higher education is a right or a privilege.

As president of a public university I have been led to ponder anew the meaning of higher education in our society, or more accurately, the public's perception of the role of higher education in U.S. society. We know that many parents and decision makers think of universities as places that should be primarily engaged in job training – preparing people for more productive and lucrative careers. Understanding that interest, how do we effectively convey to the public our concern about the general enlightenment of students, about their readiness for productive and responsible citizenship in addition to their vocational or professional preparation? How do we balance our responsibility for elevating the spirit, for advocating learning for its own sake, and for the general enlightenment of our charges, with our responsibility for training competent practitioners for business and the professions?

Over the past fifty years, perhaps partly because of the influence of the GI Bill, Americans have come to consider higher education as a right. That

---

[27]   See *College Is Possible* website <http://www.collegeispossible.org/>.

[28]   See *College is Possible* <http://www.collegeispossible.org/paying/financial.htm>.

would seem to be at the heart of the outcry about rising costs. But if higher education is a right, for what purpose? Is it a societal right because it functions for the public good, or can we in good conscience claim it a "right" for our private benefit? If our current thinking is that every American has a right to college access, and that the public has some responsibility through various governmental mechanisms to help pay for that ideal, then isn't it appropriate to ask in what ways the public good must be served? How do we distinguish between what is public good and what is private benefit? Over the years, as access and upward mobility have been emphasized, American universities have become well known and highly regarded internationally for the way in which we have combined liberal learning with practical preparation for careers. But where does public responsibility end and private investment begin?

As state support declines, we are forced to consider more and more that preparation for a profession is a private investment. Should the public pay for a student's vocational or career preparation? Or, more appropriately, shouldn't the student be expected to make at least part of that investment him- or herself? Could we assert that an individual who expects access to U.S. institutions of higher learning also be reminded about his or her *service* commitment to society? In other words, if the emphasis is going to remain on mobility for the individual while at the same time answering the calls of business, legislature, and citizenry, should then part of the service component be the subsidizing of one's education to help alleviate the tax burden on society?

A college education, after all, is an investment, not just a cost. Individuals will benefit throughout their lives from two distinct aspects of a college education. Everyone understands the instrumental element – preparation for the work place. That is to some extent for the public good, surely; but it is certainly for private benefit also. The other aspect is clearly for the public good: enlightenment. This includes sensitivity to issues that advance civilization. That aspect, which we call liberal education, or – as one of our senior professors prefers to call it, *liberating* education – must be protected, advocated, and advanced by those of us to whom the society has entrusted academic leadership.

So, in my opinion, serving the public good by a commitment to "liberating education" is our responsibility as an institution of higher learning, in keeping with the dual aspect of mobility and service. As demands for access increase, and with it expectations of continued upward mobility in America and elsewhere, education, increasingly, must be viewed as a shared responsibility. This, alas, includes cost.

The issue of cost will continue to be one of our greatest challenges. Criticism about increasing cost is in part a result of a greater percentage of the populace who aspire to be our clients, because increasing numbers dilute the state's contribution for the benefit of any given individual. And, in considering the collective benefit, too few people give thought to the service role that has defined America through the ages. Our students, their parents, and the elected officials who represent them must ponder how important higher education is to the future of our state and nation – to a state's economy in the wake of increased global competition, to be sure, but also to the nation's legacy of *prosperity balanced by service.* They might begin by dwelling more on that service component, on the enlightenment and cultural enrichment of a nation whose citizens feel threatened by incivility and social breakdown. They might dwell more on their own patriotic responsibility to defend certain values, even definitions, of what "higher education" means.

It is incumbent upon us not only to address questions about cost, emphasizing service as much as mobility, but also to report our response more publicly. This brings up the issue of accountability. In America, we are operating in an age of accountability, not just in higher education, of course, but in most aspects of contemporary society. Immediate access to information of all types drives the zeal for accountability, but whatever the reason, the pressure for it is with us and will stay with us. Most states in the U.S. have gone through some form of accountability reporting for their public institutions of higher education. Consequently, university presidents like myself have the obligation to face this challenge by framing the questions that will be put to us, again emphasizing service as much as mobility. Questions about mobility – advancement of one's career – are easily quantifiable. The responses are stated in degrees granted, jobs attained, average beginning salaries for graduates, and so forth. Accountability questions concerning service are more elusive because they can only be answered *qualitatively.*

In their attempts toward greater accountability for public higher education, most states in the U.S. have not asked important questions, which defy quantitative answers, such as how we know whether a student has achieved what we expected of him or her. We recognize, of course, many important and lasting influences of higher education that are very difficult to measure in any precise way. For example, when I spoke to all of our entering first-year students at the beginning of this academic year, I told them what I would consider to be success in their university experience. I said that both they and the university will be successful if they develop a learning habit. I told them, "success will be…
– when you have learned how to learn and enjoy doing it;

– when you have curiosity about all sorts of things around you ...
    a curiosity that makes you want to know more;
– when you're not content just to get an assignment done, but want to complete
    it to the very best of your ability;
– when you encounter a problem and realize that you can't even suggest a
    solution until you know the facts about it;
– when you not only know the facts but can synthesize and apply them."

I think one might agree that those are laudable goals, but how are they to
be measured with any degree of precision that can be reported to the general
public or to any others who would hold us accountable? If we look at all that
we do in higher education, it seems to me that the most important questions
– such as whether we have inspired creativity or triggered inquiring minds –
are the most difficult to answer. The most meaningful answers are not neat
and so cannot be expressed in numbers. Rather, the answers to accountability
questions that are most important to us in academia might be stated as *examples*
that we recognize as valid indicators of our success, such as:

– the teacher with a zeal to keep learning;
– the meticulously curious researcher in the laboratory;
– the public displays of our artists;
– the social concern of our outreach;
– the mutual respect and internal morale in a learning community.

One might note that the answers to questions such as these reaffirm education's service commitment, without which higher education in America cannot
flourish as it has now for more than two centuries. As we sign agreements
with institutions in other parts of the globe to share people and information,
technology and techniques, institutions like my Ohio University have a moral
obligation to emphasize service as it appears in our charter, for the prosperity
of a *global* society as well as the individual. And as society becomes increasingly global and electronic, we owe it to our educational partners not only to
share the keys of our funding mechanisms but also the principles upon which
our economies are based: mobility balanced by service, opportunity offset by
contribution, prosperity ensured via civic virtue ... for the individual and for
the collective good.

INTERNET SOURCES OF INFORMATION ABOUT U.S. HIGHER EDUCATION

http://nces.ed.gov/pubs/digest97/listtables.html

List of Tables for the *Digest of Education Statistics 1997*. Lists 422 tables in all (for all levels of education).

http://www.collegeispossible.org/

"A Resource Guide for Parents, Students, and Education Professionals." Includes sections on "Preparing for College," "Choosing the Right College," and "Paying for College."

http://www.collegeboard.org/

Information about a full range of information and services of The College Board, publishers the Scholastic Aptitude Tests (SAT), the Advanced Placement (AP) examinations, the College-Level Examination Program (CLEP, for students to earn college credits by examination).

http://www.collegeboard.org/policy/html/paindx000.html

Policy Analysis and Research section of the College Board site, above.

http://nces.ed.gov/index.html

Home page for the National Center for Education Statistics. Vast amounts of information available on all facets of education in the United States.

http://www.acenet.edu/

Home page for the American Council on Education, the "umbrella organization" for U.S. higher education. Valuable for up-to-date news about U.S. government legislation and policy regarding higher education.

http://ericir.sunsite.syr.edu/

Access to a "virtual library" of information about education, the Educational Resources Information Center (ERIC), a federally-funded national information system that provides, through 16 subject-specific clearinghouses, associated adjunct clearinghouses, and support components, a variety of services and products on a broad range of education-related issues. This site is specifically for AskERIC, "a personalized Internet-based service providing education information to teachers, librarians, counselors, administrators, parents, and others throughout the United States and the world."

http://www.ed.gov/

Home page for the U.S. Department of Education – information about all federal government programs and policies regarding education in the U.S.

http://www.aacrao.com/policy/govrel/index.html

Government Relations section of the web site for the American Association of Collegiate Registrars and Admissions Officers (AACRAO) – provides timely information on policy issues.

Diversifying the Pool of Faculty, Staff and Students in the Academic Setting: Who Benefits and Why?

C. Aisha BLACKSHIRE-BELAY

The following discussion is devoted to the American context with the unspoken understanding that many/most of the issues discussed are not peculiar to the United States alone. This paper might therefore also have been entitled: "Views and Perspectives on Diversity in the German and American Institutions of Higher Education." As an African American woman, having spent a relatively large portion of my academic life in both Germany and the United States, I hope that my contribution will be both unique and special in many ways.

Diversity in education is the quality of creating and sustaining curricula, academic activities, programs, and projects that actively enhance respect for all human cultures. Seeking a diverse academy does not portend the disuniting of America; to the contrary, it suggests the possibility that a multiplicity of self-respecting and other-respecting cultures could co-exist in a more perfect union. In fact, the only way that diverse cultures can co-exist for long is on the basis of such mutual appreciation and respect. Thus, diversity in the curriculum is one way to support the objective of an effective education for the twenty-first century when our colleges and universities will be infinitely more diverse than they are today. However, it is not diversity itself that should encourage multiculturalism but our commitment as human beings to the fullest possible

C. Aisha BLACKSHIRE-BELAY: Professor and Chair of African and African American Studies at Indiana State University; former Professor at Temple University and Ohio State University; Visiting Research Scholar in Bénin, Togo, Cameroon, Munich, and Berlin; specialized in comparative linguistics, language contact, diversity issues in national and international contexts. Her publications include books and articles on African-German experience, German history and culture, African American language and literature, second language acquisition and development, verb morphology in German of foreign workers.

appreciation of other cultures. So it does not matter whether the college is located in Munich, Germany, or an all-white town in the state of Indiana, the imperatives for multiculturalism are based on the concrete values of human cultural experiences.

In the 1998 findings of the first-ever national poll on diversity in higher education, conducted by Daniel Yankelovich's firm, DYG Inc. for the Ford Foundation's Campus Diversity Initiative [1] the President of the Association of American Colleges and Universities, Ms. Carol Geary Schneider, stated that "Higher education fulfills a need by creating spaces where people from diverse backgrounds learn from and with one another. Also, diversity challenges educators and students alike to reexamine our most fundamental assumptions. Above all, diversity asks us to address the links between education and a developed sense of responsibility to one another."

According to the poll, Americans see many benefits to diversity in higher education:

- Two in three Americans say it is very important that colleges and universities prepare people to function in a diverse society.
- Fifty-five percent say that every college student should have to study different cultures in order to graduate.
- By a margin of more than three to one, those who have an opinion say that diversity programs in colleges and universities raise rather than lower academic standards.
- Nearly three in five (58 percent) say our nation is growing apart, and 71 percent say that diversity education on college and university campuses helps bring society together.

"This poll shows that, despite the heated public debate over diversity, Americans are very clear in their views," said Alison R. Bernstein, a Ford Foundation Vice President. "They support diversity in higher education. They recognize that diversity is important to student success. And they believe that diversity education can help bring the country together."

A college education must address racial, ethnic, international and geographic diversity, said University of Michigan President Lee C. Bollinger. "There are all kinds of diversity, and it's critical that our students come to terms with differences."

Other findings from the DYG, Inc. poll were:

---

[1]   The Ford Foundation's Campus Diversity Initiative is a partnership with American colleges and universities to promote understanding of cultural diversity as a resource for learning.

- Ninety-seven percent of respondents agree that "in the next generations, people will need to get along with people who are not like them." Ninety-four percent agree that the "nation's growing diversity makes it more important than ever for all of us to understand people who are different from ourselves."
- Just one in five Americans (22 percent) say the nation is doing a good job of preparing itself to meet the challenges that lie ahead.
- By a margin of more than three to one, respondents say that diversity education does more to bring society together (71 percent) than drive society apart (19 percent). Ninety-one percent agree that "our society is multi-cultural and the more we know about each other, the better we will get along."
  Clear majorities say that:
- diversity on campus has a more positive (69 percent) than negative (22 percent) effect on the general atmosphere on college campuses;
- having a diverse student body has a more positive (75 percent) than negative (18 percent) effect on the education of students; and
- courses and campus activities that emphasize diversity and diverse perspectives have more of a positive (69 percent) than negative (22 percent) effect on the education of students.

Two-thirds (66 percent) say that colleges and universities should take explicit steps to insure diversity in the student body; 75 percent say that colleges and universities should take explicit steps to insure diversity among faculty. Thirty-eight percent agree and 52 percent disagree that diversity is used as an excuse to admit and graduate students who wouldn't otherwise make it.

Nine in ten (91 percent) agree that the global economy makes it more important than ever for all of us to understand people who are different than ourselves. Ninety-four percent say it is important for colleges and universities to prepare people to function in a more diverse work force.

Eighty-eight percent support offering courses in business schools on managing a diverse work force.

One in three respondents (34 percent) say that "diversity education is nothing more than political correctness, which hinders true education." More than half (58 percent) agree that "diversity education always seems to have a liberal political agenda."

The factors that limit access to higher education and reduce diversity affect professors as well as students. We must force ourselves to look at the economic, racial, and cultural barriers that make it so hard for America's colleges and universities to deliver on the American dream. Or put another way, for everyone to do the right thing by those who have been denied access for so long. If we are ever to emerge our nation's racial dilemma, we must learn to deal with the pain it has caused–in the academic community as elsewhere.

What I know now, if I did not realize it before, is that there is no clear path to a multicultural education. However, I am as convinced as I have always been that it is one of the most positive ways to bring about a greater sense of collective responsibility. I am convinced that America is a dynamic project; it is not a static idea and neither is the American university a static institution despite the entrenched attitudes supportive of a monoethnic and monocultural response to a multicultural society.

Among the difficulties in our society are the minimizing of other cultural traditions, the obliteration of histories, the promotion of patriarchy, and the elevation of the material reality at the expense of the spiritual or relational. Understanding the European American experience as a normal player on the field with other cultures is the great problem of anti-multiculturalists. They seem to insist on white American history and culture over all without reference to the agency that exists in other cultures. Thus, the demand that African Americans, Latinos, Asians, and First Americans "become" white in attitude, tastes, opinion, and behavior is not only an imposition but an oppressive idea when forced by curriculum, process, or a system of rewards and punishment where whites reward those who deny their own heritage or culture and punish those who are most "centered." This particular situation is often referred to by African Americans as the "double sickness" where whites reinforce African Americans in our insanity. That is, the farther a person is from his or her personal cultural center the more recognition and acceptance by the white university; the closer a person is to his or her culture, the less the acceptance in the university. In fact, many African Americans who wear African clothes or braid their hair in Egyptian braids have been met with hostility from their white colleagues. Consequently, many African Americans, understanding the career dynamics of racism within the academy seek to imitate European ideals in dress, tastes, vocal accents, and mannerisms in order to gain access to advancement. They are victims of a sinister hegemony which seeks, not to celebrate, but to eliminate cultures in order to claim multiculturalism.

America has always been multi-ethnic and multicultural. This was so when there were only Iroquois, Muskogee, Lakota, and Algonquin people on the land. There is no other origin nor any other destiny of this land. The same cannot be said for higher education. It originated in denial of the African and indigenous people and was not designed to educate our people, for often inherent in those early curricula were the seeds of white supremacy not multiculturalism. Furthermore, the education granted to white males, its first students, was really about white cultural assertion over the darker ethnic groups and the celebration of white cultural esteem. By the time the institutions got around to accepting women, Africans, and First Americans, they were proficient at a curriculum that would make of Africans and First Americans a class who could interpret law, literature, science, history, and even their own oppression in the interests of whites. The idea, rarely expressed but dutifully executed, was to create a class of persons, African or First American in blood and skin color, but white in values, habits, morals, and in intellect. Prosecution of this line of thinking was to prove immensely popular particularly to an African people so desirous of education that they were willing to abandon even the little that they remembered for the idea of American education. This was not quite so successful among the First Americans who saw very early the danger of receiving an education that would make them leery of their own people, spiteful of their own heroes, and antagonists of their own cultural and economic interests.

Diversity brings the real world into the classroom. It extends academic freedom by broadening the range of ideas acceptable on the nation's campuses. In this paper I provide you with information on several key areas of the discussion on diversity in the university setting:

1. Brief discussion on the issue of Affirmative Action;
2. The scant presence of minority students and faculty on campuses;
3. The representation of women; and
4. Suggestions and possible solutions.

1. Affirmative Action

Affirmative action was designed to guarantee representation of minorities and women in the work force according to their numbers and qualifications. Such procedures acknowledge that people are not hired simply on the basis of their qualifications. Many individuals have an unfair advantage in employment, housing, education, and so on, because of their membership in a particular group. Although affirmative action has been misperceived as making employers hire a minority candidate or a woman over a more qualified white person, it in fact ensures the hiring of minority candidates who are more qualified than their white competitors, and serves to give them a fair shake. It also gives hiring possibilities to minority candidates who are as qualified as qualified white applicants. The goal is a work force in which no group is over represented. In the United States many white Americans simply refuse to acknowledge the fact that all white Americans were provided with privilege under the racist system of Jim Crow – before the passing of the Affirmative Action Bill in 1965, the court decision of Plessey vs. Ferguson in 1896, the policy of segregation separate but equal was legally declared. Today there are no longer "for whites only" signs, no doors closed that you are aware of. It is not blatant racism that I am referring to here, but racism is institutionalized, deeply embedded in the system itself.

Affirmative action, implemented correctly, brings in excellent workers who would have otherwise been kept out of the system. Many unqualified people are hired every day without affirmative action. It is not a perfect system, but until we come up with something better to eliminate prejudices, discriminatory practices, and racism, our only choice is to ensure that affirmative action is implemented properly.

But the debate over the empirical consequences of affirmative action–that is, how long it will take to even out the proportions of second-rate blacks and whites–is most striking for its high ration of claims to evidence. We have little systematic knowledge of whether highly placed blacks feel more insecure about their capabilities than do highly placed whites or whether they interpret what insecurity they feel in racial terms. Evidence is just as scarce on whether whites denigrate highly placed blacks presumably aided by affirmative action, or whether such appointees overcome initial skepticism by demonstrated accomplishments or mere habituation.

Anecdotes pull in equal but opposite directions. On the one hand is the Detroit Symphony Orchestra, which responded to pressure for more racial diversity by hiring a substitute black bass player rather than holding the usual blind auditions. The bassist took the job but "would have rather auditioned like everybody else. Somehow this devalues the audition and worth of every other player." A black assistant conductor was equally torn: "Now even when a black player is hired on the merits of his playing he will always have the stigma that it was to appease some state legislator."

Quoting from Professor Henry Louis Gates,[2] "It will take till eternity for the number of second-rate blacks in the university to match the number of second-rate whites."

---

[2]   Professor and Chairman in the Department of African American Studies at Harvard University in Cambridge, Massachusetts.

2. The Scant Presence of Minority Students and Faculty

More than 30 years have passed since the enactment of the 1964 Civil Rights Act, and higher education has made real progress in opening up our nation's campuses to minority students. For example, in 1960 there were only 150,000 black students in higher education; by 1975 that number had risen to approximately one million. But progress since then has slowed, and national commitment to equality and access seems to have faltered. Enrollments of black students have remained stagnant since 1975. This is not to say that institutions have failed to address the problem; indeed, campuses across the nation have put in place a variety of programs and policies to promote the recruitment and retention of minority students, faculty, and staff. However, these efforts have not produced sustained success. The gap between the participation rates of white students and minority students is growing, and attrition is a major problem. What, then, has gone wrong? Why haven't these efforts worked?

There are several possible answers to this question. The first relates to the importance of sustained efforts to improve primary and secondary schools. African American, Latino and Chicano students are more likely to be poor. Heavily concentrated in urban city public schools, they frequently receive an education inferior to that of more affluent and white students. Native American youngsters have a far lower graduation rate from high school than African Americans, Latinos and Chicanos. They, too, are handicapped by poor preparation. Students who come ill-prepared to college begin at a disadvantage, and may never catch up.

The national movement to improve primary and secondary schools in the United States has gained considerable momentum in the last twenty years. Higher education institutions have joined this effort by working with public schools to reduce the pool of unprepared students; these initiatives will require time to bear fruit. A sustained and serious school reform movement may have its real payoff in 5, 10, or 20 years.

A second reason for the lack of progress is the piecemeal approach many institutions have taken to increasing minority participation. Isolated programs to attract and retain minority students, faculty and staff keep the effort marginal to the central mission of the institution. Comprehensive, institution-wide policies and programs, nourished by vigorous leadership from the president and the governing board, are key to institutional change. Real progress requires that increasing diversity be an integral part of the institution's mission, its planning process, and its day-to-day activities.

Another reason is that academe is simply slow to change. Creating a truly pluralistic campus requires profound change, both on a personal and organizational level. Human nature instinctively resists such change when the status quo is comfortable. The intrinsic rewards of justice for disenfranchised groups of citizens, or the necessity of adaptation to a new demographic reality may seem remote to the average faculty or board member. Some members of the academic community simply do not see the urgency of this issue for their lives, or their campuses.

MINORITY STUDENTS

Let us briefly examine the problem we are facing nationally. What have the trends been in enrollment and graduation of minority students? In the attainment of advanced degrees by African Americans, Latino, Chicano and Native Americans? What is the magnitude of the task that lies ahead?

As the following data illustrate, the issue of minority participation is a continuum; every phase is linked to the previous and the succeeding one. Consider these facts about minority students:

– Higher education's pool of students is increasingly made up of minority youth. In 25 of our largest cities and metropolitan areas, half of the public school students come from minority groups. In 1985, 20 percent of the school-age population was minority; in the year 2020, that figure will rise to 39 percent.

– College attendance by black students has slowed; the gap in participation between whites and blacks is growing. Between 1967 and 1975, the percentage of black high school graduates 24 years old and younger who were enrolled in or had completed one or more years of college rose from 35 percent to 48 percent; over the same period, the corresponding rate for whites grew much more slowly from 51 to 53 percent. However, between 1975 and 1985, while the college participation rate for white youths continued to climb to 55 percent, the rate for blacks dropped to 44 percent. Recently released figures indicate that, in 1986, the rate for blacks rose to 47 percent.

– The rate of college attendance for Chicano and Latino youths has declined in the last decade. While the number of Chicano and Latino students enrolled in college has increased significantly since 1975, the rate of attendance declined slightly between 1975 and 1985, from 51 percent to 47 percent.

– College attendance by American Indian students lags far behind black and Chicano and Latino attendance. A recent report by the Cherokee Nation found that only 55 percent of Native Americans graduate from high school, and of these, only 17 percent go on to college.

- Minority students are concentrated in community colleges. In the Fall of 1986, over 55 percent of the Latinos and Chicanos and just over 43 percent of the African Americans attending college were enrolled in two-year institutions. Few of these students ever go on to attend or graduate from four-year institutions.
- Black, Latino and Chicano are far less likely than white students to complete a degree. Among 1980 high school seniors who enrolled in college, 21 percent of the white students, compared with 10 percent of the black students and 7 percent of the Latino and Chicano students, earned a bachelor's degree or higher degree by Spring 1986.
- Blacks attending historically black colleges and universities (HBCUs) are more likely to complete a degree than those attending predominantly white institutions. In 1984 – 85, HBCUs awarded 34 percent of baccalaureate degrees earned by blacks while enrolling 18 percent of black students.
- Black, Latino and Chicano participation in graduate and professional education can best be described as minuscule in the areas of mathematics and the sciences. Though the patterns are shifting, minority students are still heavily concentrated in education. In 1986, 462 blacks earned doctorates in education, but only 6 in mathematics and 8 in physics. Latinos and Chicanos earned 188 in education, 12 in mathematics, and 15 in physics; Native Americans earned 26 doctorates in education, one in mathematics and none in physics. [3]

MINORITY FACULTY

The numbers are even more disheartening for minority faculty members and administrators. And numbers do not tell the whole story. Episodes of racially motivated violence or conflict on campus, the social and academic difficulties faced by black, Latino, Asian, Chicano and Native American students, faculty, and staff indicate that there is much work to be done to create a pluralistic and welcoming educational environment for all.

For many faculty, particularly those who favor research over teaching, securing a faculty position at a major research institutions is a dream come true. These universities, of which there are 120 nationwide, offer some of the most ideal conditions available for the pursuit of scholarly and scientific research.

Research institutions employ roughly one quarter of the faculty working at four-year institutions and produce roughly three-quarters of all Ph.D. scholars. They produce 61 percent of all African American doctorates and 76 percent

---

[3]   *Minority Students on American College Campuses.* Working Papers by the Department of African and African American Studies, Indiana State University.

of all Latino doctorates. Nevertheless, African American and Latino faculty, particularly those with tenure or on a tenure-track appointment, continue to be scarce at research institutions.

African American and Latino scholars, of which there are 5,278 and 3,318 respectively at research institutions, constitute only 5.2 percent of the 163,548 faculty at these universities. Among faculty with tenure (119,838), only 2.9 percent are African American (3,479), and 1.9 percent (2,326) are Latino.

The numbers analysis that I am providing here, which is based upon data collected by the U.S. Department of Education, paints a detailed portrait of where African American and Latino scholars are within the nation's research institutions. It also offers insights on how these schools are performing in relationship to one another with respect to minority faculty recruitment and retention. For example, the percentage of tenured/tenure-track minority faculty at research institutions in 1995 provided us with the following figures: 2.9% African American and 1.9% Latino tenured/tenure-track faculty.

The future of our nation is inextricably tied to an educated population that can contribute to the labor force and the economy, as well as to our national well-being. If one-third of the nation will be composed of minority persons by the year 2010, as the demographers predict, minority citizens must be included in the economic, political, social, and educational mainstream.

Higher education has a vital role to play, both as a force for social justice and in producing an educated and productive citizenry. Our future as a nation depends on our ability to reverse these downward trends in minority achievement in education and ensure that our campuses are as diverse as our country. We cannot afford to defer the dream of full participation by all citizens; it is not only unjust, but unwise.

3. Representation of Women

There is a lack of representation at the top levels in the academy. Invisible factors, as much as or more so than overt discrimination, keep women from rising to the top.

Discrepancies between men's and women's salaries occur both in the business world and in academia. Women tend to benefit less from their qualifications than men do. In many cases, women's human capital–their training, years of job experience, and so on–is less than men's. But even when men and women are equal in human capital, or when their differences are statistically equalized, men get more from their investment than women do.

In academia men and women now start out with equal salaries, but they do not progress at the same pace. Data from the National Science Foundation for 1993 showed that full-time academic male and female scientists were close to parity in their salaries one to two years after they received their Ph.D.'s. But three to eight years after completing the Ph.D., women earned 92 percent of men's salaries, and at nine to thirteen years afterward, women earned only 90 percent of their male counterparts' salaries.

Also, in terms of leadership, women are not given credit. Gender schemas not only make it difficult for women to be evaluated accurately; they also make it difficult for women to reap the benefits of their achievements and be recognized as leaders.

Failing to label a woman seated at the head of a table as a leader may have no discriminatory impetus behind it. But a woman leader is nevertheless prone to lose out compared with a man in the same position, because she is less likely to receive the automatic deference that marks of leadership confer on men. As a result, the woman is objectively hurt even if observers intend no hurt. She has to work harder to be seen as a leader.

4. Suggestions and Possible Solutions

The institutions that have been successful in improving minority participation have at least one important characteristic in common: *They have developed a comprehensive and institution-wide approach.* Too often in the past, institutions have tried a program here, a new staff person there. An institution-wide commitment to enhancing diversity and vigorous leadership from the chief executive officer and the governing board will produce more qualitatively different results than an institution undertaking sporadic and piecemeal efforts, even if they are well conceived and well executed.

A comprehensive approach requires institution-wide planning and coordination. Improving minority participation becomes a goal for all departments and academic units, a factor in the strategic planning process, a criterion by which individuals and units are evaluated. All involved must understand how the pieces fit together, and how their own roles and responsibilities relate to the whole.

Strategies for Success

While strategies will vary from campus to campus, there are certain constants that undergird successful efforts.

Leadership from the top. It is important that governing boards and chief executive officers be fully committed to the goal of enhancing minority participation and that this commitment be demonstrated in word and deed. Statements of purpose and commitment issued by the board and/or president are important beginnings, both symbolically and actually. Diversity on the board, on the presidents' staff, the celebration of diversity in all aspects of campus life, and the clear willingness to allocate resources to achieve equity are but a few concrete demonstrations of leadership.

Leadership from the ranks. While the commitment of the board and president are important, they cannot accomplish real change without support and leadership throughout the institution. For example, any individual hiring a new staff member can actively recruit minority candidates by contacting colleagues at other institutions for suggestions rather than simply relying on responses to advertisements. Similarly, department chairs play a key role in developing strategies to recruit minority graduate students through networks in their own discipline. Faculty involvement in all phases of institutional planning and implementation is crucial. In short, institutional change is the sum of many individual actions.

Involvement of minority persons. While this sounds obvious, it is a crucial point. The planning effort will be sound or successful only with the input of affected groups and with their participation in the formulation of the agenda and potential solutions.

Support of minority networks. Networks of minority students, faculty, and staff are key to providing them with information and support. Institutional leaders can support these networks by providing resources and recognition.

Mentoring for students, faculty, and staff. An advisor and an advocate will help all individuals grow personally and professionally as well as learn the system. Mentoring programs are especially useful to minority individuals to develop relationships with both majority and minority colleagues and to be sure that they have advisors and advocates.

Allocation of sufficient resources. Find the money to achieve your objectives may mean that something else is not done. Discussions and decisions regarding allocation of resources to minority concerns must be incorporated into the ongoing institutional planning process.

Provision of incentives. People need encouragement and rewards to change. Incentives may be as abstract as encouragement and public recognition of accomplishments. Or, they may be as concrete as awarding extra faculty positions, extra departmental resources, or including criteria for performance appraisals that are related to the goals of improving minority participation. If necessary, sanctions can be applied to those individuals or units that are unco-operative.

Explicit and result-oriented efforts. It is important that the main goals be translated at every stage into short-term goals that are easily identified and understood. Some efforts will be easily quantifiable. For example, you might decide to increase new minority freshmen five percent over two years or hire one minority faculty member during that time period. Other, more qualita-tive changes will need to be broken down into a series of defined steps. For example, improving campus climate may include an institutional audit, iden-tification of problem areas, and suggested strategies for each area, followed by reassessment. Specific outcomes, quantitative and/or qualitative, should be identified for all targets of institutional change. Progress must be regularly as-sessed against the yardstick of your desired outcomes. Appropriate schedules for meeting these targets should be established.

A good complaint system. A formal grievance procedure to handle dis-crimination or harassment complaints is essential. But many people prefer in-formal dispute resolution for most (but not all) problems. Most people would rather deal with the problem and arrive at a satisfying solution than "win the case." The informal complaint system or process will be structured differently on different campuses. For example, there may be a specially designated om-budsperson, or a task force charged with the responsibility. One hopes that most disputes will be resolved in the work group.

Manageable goals. Most would agree that change in the academy is of-ten difficult and slow. Thus, it is helpful to think big, but start small, setting goals that can be reasonably attained. A steady stream of incremental changes will have an enduring impact. It is important to monitor progress toward the goals to keep to your schedule. Period evaluation may warrant adjustment and modification of your goals.

Periodic reporting to the president and governing board.

CONCLUSION

Greater minority participation will improve the quality of campus life for all. All students will benefit as the curriculum is broadened and different perspec-tives are introduced and as the teaching and learning processes are adapted to meet different learning styles. The presence of minority faculty can serve to inspire students to achieve as well as to introduce faculty colleagues to new perspectives. Many institutions have begun the effort to make their campuses truly reflective of the rich diversity of the United States. No one has all the answers; there is no sure-fire recipe for success, but a diverse body of faculty, students, administrators and staff is essential to improve all of our lives and making the world a better place.

WOMEN AT GERMAN UNIVERSITIES: A CASE OF NON-DIVERSIFICATION?

Silvia MERGENTHAL

In 1897, the journalist Arthur Kirchhoff edited a collection of articles entitled *Die Akademische Frau. Gutachten hervorragender Universitätsprofessoren, Frauenlehrer und Schriftsteller über die Befähigung der Frau zum wissenschaftlichen Studium und Berufe.* [1] Kirchhoff had asked 122 eminent professors, teachers, and writers whether, in their opinion, women should be admitted to German universities as students (given that, for the preceding three decades, they had been campaigning for access to secondary and tertiary educational institutions), and whether, having successfully completed their courses of study, women might even become professors themselves. About half of Kirchhoff's respondents were vociferous in their opposition to women in academia, claiming that women were constitutionally incapable of sustained intellectual work. Among the other half, support for the cause of women's higher education was mostly lukewarm and hedged with cautionary tales, and there were only very few contributors who argued, as did the Erlangen professor of medicine Isidor Rosenthal, that, although boys (unlike girls) had been subjected to rigorous training for centuries, only a small percentage of *men* were cut out to become professors. In his introductory comments, Kirchhoff attributed this unfavourable response to the fact that women academics did not comply with traditional gender roles, but he regarded these gender roles as obsolete, and men's conservative attitude towards them as selfish.

Silvia MERGENTHAL: Professor of English and American Literature at the Universität Konstanz, she is Commissioner for Women, coordinates the Gender Studies program, and serves as a member of the Baden-Württemberg Commission for Improving Women Studies; she has published in the areas of gender studies, Scottish literature, contemporary British literature and postcolonial literatures.

[1] Berlin: Steinitz; quoted in Abele-Brehm, Andrea, "Frauen an der Friedrich-Alexander-Universität," *Stieftöchter der Alma Mater? 90 Jahre Frauenstudium in Bayern am Beispiel der Universität München. Katalog zum Erlanger Sonderteil der Ausstellung*, ed. Frauenbeauftragte der Friedrich-Alexander-Universität (Erlangen: Eigenverlag, 1996), 11–22.

Three years later, the first women students were officially allowed to enroll at universities in Baden (education being, then as now, a prerogative of the individual German states rather than of the federal government), and Bavaria followed suit in 1903. By international standards, German women students were late-comers on the academic scene: American and Russian universities had opened their doors to women as early as 1860, French universities in 1863, and Swiss universities in 1864.

Over a hundred years after Kirchhoff's publication, nearly 50 percent of students at German universities are women, but women fill less than 10 per cent of all the professorial posts, and less than 5 percent of the most prestigious (C 4) posts. These figures, as well as the graphs and statistics given in the 1998 *Wissenschaftsrat* [2]. Equal Opportunities Recommendations reprinted in the appendix to this paper, document what amounts to a continuing marginalization of women in German universities. If one takes those subjects which attract the highest percentage of female students as an example, namely, those broadly termed humanities, we start out with 65 percent female students, but a comparatively much higher percentage of their male fellow students will successfully complete a Ph.D., the ratio here being 42 female to 58 male candidates. On the level of *Habilitation*, the level drops to 26 percent, and only 15 percent of all the professors in the humanities are women. Statistically speaking, these women are more likely to find themselves in C2 and C3 posts, as, across all the subjects, only four per cent of university chairs, C 4, are held by women. If women do find employment within the university, it is less in tenure track but rather in, as it were, tenuous, that is, part-time and adjunct positions. One could, of course, argue that the percentages are indicative of impending change, i.e. of women slowly moving upwards into the higher ranks of the profession, but unfortunately, the figures, at least with regard to the humanities, have remained fairly constant over the last couple of decades. In other words, given the figures of the early 80s, with roughly 60 percent female students, surely a larger percentage should have climbed the academic career ladder. So, why haven't they?

If one assumes, rightly, I think, that German society as a whole is not intrinsically more misogynist than other societies, one needs to find other factors which militate against career opportunities for women within the university system. The most important among these factors seems to be, according to the Wissenschaftsrat publication already mentioned, the virtual absence of a ca-

---

[2] *Empfehlungen zur Chancengleichheit von Frauen in Wissenschaft und Forschung*, dated May 15, 1999.

reer structure after the first degree. If one compares the German system to an obstacle course, the obstacles which have to be surmounted *en route* to a professorship are Ph.D., *Habilitation*, and appointment, but how one finds one's way from one obstacle to the other, or, indeed, *whether* one does, remains far from clear. Admittedly, there is one path which is particularly goal- oriented, but which is inaccessible to most: While you are still a student, one of your professors will recognize your potential, will either help you apply for grants, or offer you a teaching assistantship to get you through your Ph.D. years, will make sure you are employed as an assistant professor for six years while you do research for your *Habilitation*, and will then trade favours with one or two of the more influential members of the search committee at one of the universities where you have applied for a professorship. Even under ideal circumstances, all these stages are characterized by a high degree of insecurity and by lack of transparency.

The obvious argument now is, of course, that male candidates suffer under, and occasionally profit from, these highly inefficient recruitment processes as much as women. However, there is evidence – evidence which is difficult to quantify but which is saved from being merely anecdotal by a series of detailed, long-term surveys of women in academia – to suggest that women, at each hurdle in the obstacle course, are worse off than their male colleagues. In 1990, the sociologist Dagmar Schultz published a book entitled *Das Geschlecht läuft immer mit: Die Arbeitswelt von Professorinnen und Professoren* [3] in which she presented the results of 43 interviews conducted with 22 male and 21 female professors at three German universities. While none of the men thought that their gender had any impact on their private lives, or on their careers, every one of the women stressed this impact: they felt they were being discriminated against, subtly and in some cases distinctly unsubtly, by their male colleagues, excluded from professional networks, and burdened down with extra work, for example counseling students, and they regarded the respective claims of private (family) life and career as ultimately irreconcilable.

Schultz traces these differences in perception back to different acculturation patterns on the way to a professorial post: Male students are initiated into their chosen profession by same-sex sponsors, and even if they do not get on with these father-figures, they will see them as potential role models, and will either strive to follow in their footsteps, or to compete with them. Most male professors among Schultz's interviewees had very close relationships with se-

---

[3]   Dagmar Schultz, *Das Geschlecht läuft immer mit: Die Arbeitswelt von Professorinnen und Professoren* (Pfaffenweiler: Centaurus, 1991).

nior professors, and were supported by them to the extent of being offered
teaching assistantship or other posts. They took this support for granted, and if
they were treated unfairly by their mentors, they experienced this as an insult
which had a profoundly negative effect on their attitude towards their profession. The women, on the other hand, found the greatest support among their
own peer-group. They were intensely aware of, and grateful for, any help given
to them, however minimal, and were proud of their ability to cope with disap-
pointments and set-backs; but they had expected very little in the first place.

For female students, then, it is much more difficult to bring themselves to
the notice of their male professors, and female mentors may be hard to find,
and even if they do exist, they are quite likely to be perceived as academic outsiders. While women may well apply for Ph.D. grants nonetheless, and may
even be successful in their applications, they are far less likely to be accom-
modated, in however marginal a capacity, in their chosen department, and are
thus often excluded from professional networks. If they clear the Ph.D. obstacle, and go for a *Habilitation*, they may once again have to rely on grants rather
than find themselves with a university post, and, by now, they'll be in their late
twenties or early thirties, and become aware of the biological clock. Even with
the most supportive partner, and adequate childcare facilities, and the latter,
though perhaps not the former, are in short supply in Germany, a woman with
children will find it difficult to publish as much as her male competitors, to
spend time abroad, and to generally be as flexible in her arrangements and
as geographically mobile as they are expected to be. If, against these odds,
a woman does complete her second book, a predominantly male committee
at her home university will decide whether it is prepared to accept this as a
Habilitation, and once she starts applying for posts elsewhere, she will find
herself face to face with, again, predominantly male search committees, some
of whom will refuse to even place her on the short-list, however far down that
list, because they have succumbed to the influence of what can only be called
a modern myth, namely, that German ministers of education are so feminist
that they will appoint the woman, any woman, no matter whether the university in question wants her or not. All this can be summed up, perhaps, under
the heading "lack of encouragement and support," from within academia, and
from without. Among the female winners of the race, 60 percent are single, or
at any rate live alone, as against 19 percent of their male colleagues.

Universities have, over the last decade – or, in the case of some universities
in the north of Germany, decades – tried to improve the situation of women,
partly out of a recognition that not employing women is a sheer waste of hu-

man resources, and partly prompted by various legislative bodies; the legal frameworks for the kind of responses which will be outlined presently are, first and foremost, the German constitution, secondly, university legislation on both federal and state levels, and, finally, the constitution each university gives itself (*Grundgesetz, Hochschulrahmengesetz, Hochschulgesetz, Grundordnung*). By and large, universities throughout the country have adopted two complementary strategies, that is, they have established the office of *Frauenbeauftragte* (equal opportunities persons), and they have compiled what is normally referred to as *Frauenförderpläne*, i. e. sets of recommendations for improving the position of women within academia on all levels.

Due to the German federal system, the legal and institutional frameworks for *Frauenbeauftragte* vary greatly: they can be elected or appointed, either for a limited or an unlimited period of time; they can be full-time or honorary *Frauenbeauftragte*, their duties can extend to the university as a whole, or be restricted to individual faculties; they can be asked to represent all female members of the university, including non-academic personnel such as secretaries, librarians, laboratory technicians, or their responsibilities can be confined to female academic personnel and female students only. The Bavarian model, for example, favours the honorary *Universitätsfrauenbeauftragte*, elected by the senate of a given university from among its academic teachers for a period of two years, and supported by *Fakultätsfrauenbeauftragte* elected by the faculty councils; while they represent the teaching staff and the students, the university administration appoints a *Gleichstellungsbeauftragte* from among its non-academic employees. The actual day-to-day business of the *Universitätsfrauenbeauftragte* is conducted by so-called *Frauenbüros*. *Frauenbeauftragte* have access to virtually all the boards and committees within the university, i. e. the senate, faculty councils, search committees, and so on. They are supposed to safeguard the interests of women on every level, and to supervise the implementation of *Frauenförderpläne;* whether they can, in fact, do so effectively, is another matter and one which lies beyond the scope of this paper.

The *Handbuch für aktive Frauenarbeit an Hochschulen* of 1993 [4] provides a blueprint for a typical *Frauenförderplan*. It should include a preamble expressing the university's commitment to improving the position of women, and then touch on such issues as job advertisements and selection processes; recruitment and appointments; working hours; sabbaticals; students with fam-

---

[4]   Christine Färber, ed., *Handbuch für aktive Frauenarbeit an Hochschulen* (Marburg: Schüren, 1993).

ily responsibilities; childcare facilities; research grants; gender studies; sexual harassment, and so on. Thus, for example, the Konstanz *Frauenförderplan* recommends that, qualifications being "equal", the percentage of women teaching assistants should correspond to the percentage of women taking their first degree in a given subject, that, on the next level, the percentage of women appointed to assistant professorships should correspond to that of female Ph.D.'s. etc.; in other words, if the Faculty of Arts has seventy percent female graduates, seven out of ten, 3.5 out of 5 of the pre-Ph.D. posts should go to them, and thus all the way up the career ladder, which the figures taking from the preceding rung. Now, apart from the obvious question of how to define "equal", rather than, say, "comparable" qualifications, and the even more obvious fact that the number of posts available at any given moment is so very small that, as an administrator, you'll probably find yourself with a highly qualified woman wanting to do a Ph.D. in French, and, at best, a vacant post somewhere in the English department, the crucial problem is that all these recommendations are recommendations only, and there is no system of rewards and punishments which encourages any given administrative unit to follow these guidelines, or discourages it from not following them.

One should perhaps state unequivocally at this point, that the topic of this paper is structural, not individual or personal, discrimination. On a day-to-day basis, openly discriminatory comments such as those quoted by Schultz's female respondents tend to be much less frequent than the following: "I'd happily appoint a really good woman if only I could find one;" or: "I offered this woman a post, and now she's gone and become pregnant!" The German university system is, at this moment in time, on the brink of significant structural changes. If women have, in the past, indeed been the victims of structural discrimination, it might well be women who are going to profit most substantially from impending structural reforms.

The following suggestions for some of the directions which these reforms might take are already being discussed, and discussed controversially, from a variety of angles, and not exclusively, or even predominantly, from an equal opportunities point of view. If one does take this point of view, it will become evident that the proposed reforms might well remove some of the obstacles which, as this paper has tried to show, women still have to face within the university system.

1. There should be clearly structured Ph.D. courses, limiting the number of years students are expected to spend on a Ph.D. to three, and ensuring adequate funding-grants for this period. In the German context, this would

argue for a greater number of *Graduiertenkollege*, with students from all over the country (and, for that matter, from abroad) competing for places.

2. As a rule, every post, including teaching assistantships (*wissenschaftliche Hilfskräfte*) should be advertised, not only within a given university, but also beyond it. Appointment processes, on this and every other level, should be as transparent as possible, with job requirements outlined as clearly as possible.

3. One needs to seriously reconsider the role of *Habilitation* as a prerequisite for a professorship.

4. Finally, there should be a system of rewards and punishments. As it so happens, this system, under the heading of *evaluation*, seems likely to be put into place in the not too distant future. If, in future, universities or administrative units within universities have to compete for funds, and if funds are allocated on the grounds of their teaching and research records, their equal opportunities record may become one of the criteria of allocation.

Anteil von Frauen (in %) an den Studierenden an Universitäten (einschl. GH, Pädagogische und Theologische Hochschulen) nach Fächergruppen
ab WS 1992/93 alte und neue Länder

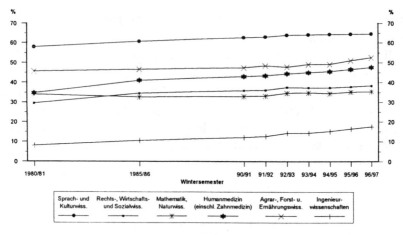

Anmerkung: Ohne Fächergruppen Kunst, Kunstwissenschaft, Sport und Veterinärmedizin. Die absoluten Zahlen sind im Vergleich zu den anderen Fächergruppen gering; eine Anteilsdarstellung würde zu einer Verzerrung des Gesamtbildes führen.

Quelle: Statistisches Bundesamt, Studierende an Hochschulen (Fachserie 11, Reihe 4.1) div. Jahrgänge.

Figure 1:

The first graph shows the percentage of female students at German universities (including teacher training colleges and theological colleges, but excluding polytechnics). The highest percentage of women students is to be found in the humanities, to be followed by the sciences (Mathematik, Naturwissenschaften), medicine (Humanmedizin, einschließlich Zahnmedizin), law/economics/social studies (Rechts-, Wirtschafts- und Sozialwissenschaften), agriculture (Agrar-, Forst- und Ernährungswissenschaften), and engineering (Ingenieurwissenschaften). Two observations should be made: the first is that, by and large, the figures have remained remarkably steady over the last two decades. The second is that the way in which subjects are grouped together in this graph obscures differences between them; thus, to take the example of the sciences, most female students will be found in biology or pharmacy, while the percentage of female students in nuclear physics will be very small.

Figure taken from: Wissenschaftsrat (ed.), *Empfehlungen zur Chancengleichheit von Frauen in Wissenschaft und Forschung* (Cologne: Wissenschaftsrat, 1998) 18.

Anteil von Frauen (in %) an den mit Erfolg abgelegten Promotionen
ab 1993 alte und neue Länder

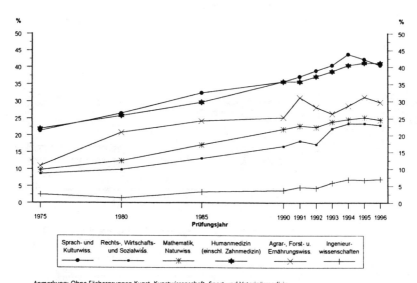

Anmerkung: Ohne Fächergruppen Kunst, Kunstwissenschaft, Sport und Veterinärmedizin.

Quelle: Statistisches Bundesamt, Prüfungen an Hochschulen (Fachserie 11, Reihe 4.2) div. Jahrgänge.

Figure 2:

The second graph shows the percentage of women among post-graduate students who have successfully completed their doctorates. The highest percentage here is, for 1996, in medicine, where a doctorate is virtually indispensable for one's further career, closely followed by the humanities. Compared to the percentages of Appendix 1, one should note that, first of all, there is a considerable rise in doctorates awarded to women in the period between 1975 and 1996; secondly, that the graphs, particularly in the areas designated Agrarwissenschaften (agriculture) and Rechtswissenschaften (law), have considerable peaks and troughs, which perhaps indicates that women are more easily influenced in their career decisions by deteriorating job prospects in their intended professions. Thirdly, while in the humanities over 65 per cent of the students are female, only just over 40 percent of humanities doctorates are held by women.

Figure taken from: Wissenschaftsrat (ed.), *Empfehlungen zur Chancengleichheit von Frauen in Wissenschaft und Forschung* (Cologne: Wissenschaftsrat, 1998) 21.

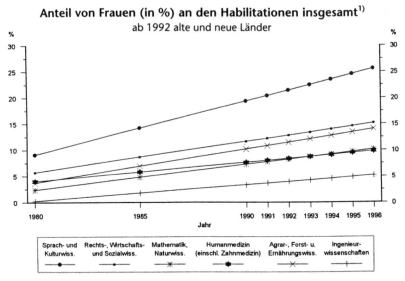

Anteil von Frauen (in %) an den Habilitationen insgesamt[1]
ab 1992 alte und neue Länder

Sprach- und Kulturwiss.	Rechts-, Wirtschafts- und Sozialwiss.	Mathematik, Naturwiss.	Humanmedizin (einschl. Zahnmedizin)	Agrar-, Forst- u. Ernährungswiss.	Ingenieur- wissenschaften
──●──	──●──	──✳──	──■──	──✕──	──+──

1) Ermittlung der Werte unter Anwendung der linearen Regressionsanalyse (ohne Fächergruppen Kunst, Kunstwissenschaft, Sport und Veterinärmedizin).

Quelle: Statistisches Bundesamt, Habilitationsstatistik

Figure 3:

The third graph shows the percentage of women among successfully completed Habilitationen. Again, there is a considerable rise, a rise which is particularly marked in the humanities; but again, we need to remind ourselves of the high percentage of female students, and the 40 percent female doctorates, to put the Habilitation figures into perspective. The only other feature worth mentioning here is the comparatively low percentage for medicine; it clearly demonstrates that, while a doctorate is indispensable for a career outside the university, it does not open the door to a career within it.

Figure taken from: Wissenschaftsrat (ed.), *Empfehlungen zur Chancengleichheit von Frauen in Wissenschaft und Forschung* (Cologne: Wissenschaftsrat, 1998) 22.

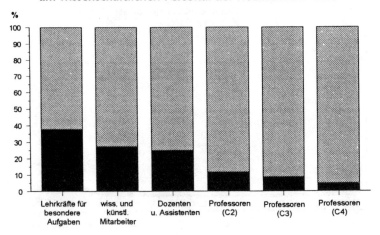

Quelle: Statistisches Bundesamt, Personal an Hochschulen 1995 (Fachserie 11, Reihe 4.4)

Figure 4:

This diagram shows the percentage of women (darker shade) in various university positions. Persons in the first column (Lehrkräfte für besondere Aufgaben) typically work in language centers, teacher training colleges etc.; these are not tenure track positions, and their job descriptions emphasize teaching (over research). Potential tenure track positions (within the German framework as outlined above) are the positions designated Dozenten und Assistenten in the third column, while the various professorships (grouped in ascending order according to salary scale) will normally guarantee tenure (and, again in the German context, civil servant status).

Figure taken from: Wissenschaftsrat (ed.), *Empfehlungen zur Chancengleichheit von Frauen in Wissenschaft und Forschung* (Cologne: Wissenschaftsrat, 1998) 23.

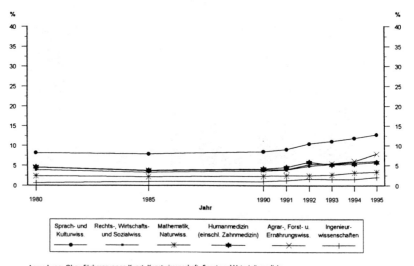

Anteil von Frauen (in %) an den Professuren der Universitäten
(einschl. Gesamthochschulen, Pädagogische und Theologische Hochschulen)
ab 1992 alte und neue Länder

Anmerkung: Ohne Fächergruppen Kunst, Kunstwissenschaft, Sport und Veterinärmedizin.

Quelle: Statistisches Bundesamt, Personal an Hochschulen (Fachserie 11, Reihe 4.4) div. Jahrgänge.

Figure 5:

While the preceding diagram has given the overall percentage of women professors, this graph
returns once again to the respective academic fields of graphs 1–3, showing, not surprisingly,
that the largest number of female professors is to be found in the humanities.

Figure taken from: Wissenschaftsrat (ed.), *Empfehlungen zur Chancengleichheit von Frauen in
Wissenschaft und Forschung* (Cologne: Wissenschaftsrat, 1998) 24.

THE AMERICAN ACADEMIC MARKETPLACE

David E. SCHINDEL

Can the American system of higher education offer any useful lessons to Germany as it considers a variety of reform efforts? At the outset I must confess that I have a relatively superficial knowledge of the German system of higher education. In my role as the National Science Foundation's (NSF) representative to all of Europe, I am expected to know at least a small amount about a large number of countries. I have learned a great deal from the presentations at the conference documented in this volume.

I believe that there are two general factors that distinguish the two systems. These factors may be cultural barriers that limit the degree to which the two systems can learn from each other. First, the American system of higher education is a competitive marketplace, and this holds true for public and private universities and colleges. In contrast, the German system is a more regulated environment. The fact that German universities are all owned and operated by the government contributes to this high level of regulation, but as the American experience demonstrates, it does not require it.

Second, the U.S. Federal government does not include any institutions devoted to fundamental research. Germany (like France and several other European countries) has a dual system of fundamental research, in which many of the best institutes for fundamental research are government labs that are not associated with universities. It is true that the U.S. Federal Government owns and operates many research institutes (e.g., Los Alamos and Sandia labs of the Department of Energy, or the Naval Research Labs), but virtually all of them are devoted to more targeted and applied research associated with the mission of that agency. Even some of these "mission-driven" Federal research labs are associated with universities (e.g., University of California, Berkeley

David SCHINDEL: Head of the National Science Foundation's (NSF) Europe Office, located at the US Embassy in Paris, and Executive Associate in the NSF Director's Office of Integrative Activities; former Professor and Curator of Invertebrate Fossils in the Yale Peabody Museum; as an invertebrate paleontologist, his research explored evolutionary theory, computer-based analysis of evolutionary change, and the role of the fossil record in shaping evolutionary theory.

hosts the Department of Energy's Lawrence Livermore Lab, and Cal Tech hosts NASA's Jet Propulsion Lab). Most of the truly fundamental research that is government-sponsored takes place in universities and colleges. This role has been given to the U.S. higher education system since after World War II, along with an ever-increasing array of Federal research grants programs. This post-War legacy, based on Vannevar Bush's blueprint *Science – the Endless Frontier* (1945)[1], has led to the growth of more than 100 research universities. More broadly, it has created a higher education system which is also the main engine for basic research in the U.S.

I will therefore devote my remarks to these two factors: competition in all aspects of higher education, and the integration of research and education within U.S. universities and colleges.

POST-WAR GROWTH AND COMPETITION

Several contributors to this volume have presented scholarly reviews of the many shared historical aspects of the two systems. The German and American systems share many basic values but their structures and behaviors have diverged remarkably during the post-War period. American colleges and universities grew extremely rapidly for a variety of reasons. Returning servicemen had the GI Bill that paid for their costs of college. American industry absorbed scientists and engineers as fast as they could be trained. Corporations, charitable foundations, and government at all levels invested in the construction of new buildings and entirely new campuses.

As this growth process accelerated, the competition for resources grew even faster. This competitive process has required that colleges and universities define and emphasize their differences and to promote these differences as strengths. In so doing, all but the largest university systems abandoned the notion of "being all things to all people." Instead, they have each tried to develop an individualistic identity as the best in a more narrowly defined category of institutions. For example, Oberlin and Antioch are two small private colleges in Ohio, but they have unmistakably different identities, and they attract different sets of students, faculty, research grants, and philanthropic donors. Graham and Diamond (1997)[2] reviewed this process of growth and differentiation and the history of attempts to rank them based on quality factors.

---

[1]   Vannevar Bush *Science – the Endless Frontier: A Report to the President* (Washington: U.S. Government Printing Office, 1945).

[2]   Hugh Davis Graham and Nancy Diamond, *The Rise of the American Research Universities: Elites and Challengers in the Postwar Era* (Baltimore: Johns Hopkins UP, 1997).

Every year, *U.S. News and World Report*[3] and many other sources publish yearly rankings of American colleges. They compare colleges based on class size, quality of the dormitories, creativity of the courses and professors, enjoyment of campus life, the ease of registering for classes, the availability of library and laboratory facilities, the difficulty of being admitted, the price of tuition and housing, the availability of financial aid, and many other factors. The validity and impact of these rankings has itself become an active research topic.[4] These ratings are debated continuously in such publications as the *Chronicle of Higher Education*. There are scores of databases on the Web with which prospective students can compare colleges before applying.

Major universities may seem outwardly more similar to each other (take the University of Michigan and the University of California-Berkeley, for example), but the similarities disappear when one compares them at a departmental level. At that level, the universities also seek to compete by differentiating themselves. By attracting faculty and developing facilities that focus on narrower topics in a particular field, a department can differentiate itself in order to compete for faculty, grants, and students. If a university department were to try to cover an entire field of research, they would likely be found mediocre in many sub- fields and thus at an overall disadvantage in the competition for resources. The U.S. National Research Council, the operational branch of the National Academies of Science, Engineering, and the Institute of Medicine, periodically publish rankings of graduate departments in the U.S. The most recent, "Research-Doctorate Programs in the United States: Continuity and Change" (1995) is available on the Web.[5]

THE UNIVERSALITY OF RISK IN AMERICAN ACADEMIA

At a variety of levels, the American system of higher education demands and promotes risk-taking. There are few areas of American academic life in which resources are distributed uniformly among applicants. Success rates are low
– for admission to college,
– for research grant applications,
– for acceptance for publication in scholarly journals,
– for appropriations from State governments,
– for requests for charitable contributions to endowment funds, and

---

[3]   <http://www.usnews.com/usnews/edu/colleg e/corank.htm>.
[4]   See research bibliography on this topic by the Education and Social Science Library, University of Illinois <http://www.library.uiuc.edu/edx/rankbib.htm>.
[5]   <http://bob.nap.edu/html/researchdoc/>.

– for hiring and promotion of faculty.

In light of these low rates of success, applicants are forced to differentiate themselves from their competitors. The high school senior applying for admission to a university is told by his or her counselor to find a "hook" that will make their application stand out from the rest. The same can be said for research grants proposals to charitable foundations and corporations, and the career development paths of young professors. But in striving to differentiate themselves from competitors, they are accepting the implicit added risk of being judged inferior, in return for the possibility of a higher than average success rate or a disproportionate share of resources.

What is the outcome of this competition? Rates of admission to the most competitive colleges can be under 10%. Scores and sometimes hundreds of qualified Ph.D.s with solid research records apply for a single assistant professor position. At major research universities, tenure is granted to fewer than one young professor in ten. The average success rate for research grant proposals at NSF is 30%, and some competitions have success rates of less than 10%. University departments can lose faculty positions due to budget cuts when another department is judged more deserving. Departments can also lose their best faculty members when they are courted by other universities offering better facilities and salaries, and more interesting colleagues and students. Small colleges go bankrupt and close every so often.

My own organization, the National Science Foundation, constantly struggles with the trade-off between the size of research grants and the proportion of successful proposals. There is a universal desire to support all worthy projects, but to do so would result in extremely small grants. None of the applicants would be able to perform world-class research with grants that were spread thinly among the majority of applicants. Knowing that a minority of proposals will receive funding, applicants must not only demonstrate the quality of their proposed projects, they must demonstrate their uniqueness and importance as well. Research grant decisions are most normally based on the last two factors.

Since the mid-1970s, the competition for resources in higher education has been increasing and universities have had to take greater risks to succeed. Recession has reduced the funding that is available from all sources. The population of college-age American students began to shrink following the peak years of education the post-War "Baby Boom." Tuition costs were rising faster than any other cost of U.S. living, including health care, and parents began to question the value of the expensive education their children were getting. The popular perception was that too many professors were spending too much of their time doing research and applying for grants, and that too many of their classes were being taught by graduate students. Many of the professors hired during the growth years of the 1950s and 60s were preparing to retire in the 1990s, and universities were facing difficult choices.

University leaders began to ask themselves: How should we prepare to compete in the realm of 21st Century research? What should we do to attract the best students during the next wave of increasing enrollment that will arrive after 2000 as a result from the "echo" of the Baby Boom? And most fundamentally, how should we divide our limited resources between our roles in education and in research?

THE INTEGRATION OF RESEARCH AND EDUCATION

The U.S. National Science Foundation has always had a dual mission to support both research and education in science and engineering. The integration of research and education in American universities was the foundation of Vannevar Bush's vision for post-War U.S. science, and it was built into the legislation that created NSF. The availability of NSF and other Federal funding agencies contributed to the growth of research universities and to a growing emphasis on research at all colleges and universities.

Universities are often criticized for supporting research at the expense of undergraduate education. The most common counter-argument is that the highest quality undergraduate education is provided by faculty scholars who are involved in active research. Virtually all of NSF-supported grants to universities and colleges seek to support both research and education simultaneously. It is difficult to find an NSF grant that doesn't combine these two missions. NSF research grants commonly include support for undergraduate and graduate students who will participate as co-investigators. Grants to improve education stress the process of moving research results and the research process into the classroom setting.

In addition to the dual nature of NSF's support through research grants and education grants, the Foundation has created numerous grants programs that focus specifically on the integration of research and education. [6] This list contains programs that seek to integrate research and education and/or programs that cut across traditional disciplinary boundaries. I would like to highlight three programs from that list – programs that exemplify the integration of re-

---

[6]   A complete listing of NSF's "Crosscutting" programs can be found on the Web at <http://www.nsf.gov/home/crssprgm/start.htm>.

search and education at the undergraduate level, at the graduate level, and at the level of entire educational institutions.

RESEARCH EXPERIENCE FOR UNDERGRADUATES

NSF encourages the Principal Investigators on research awards to include undergraduate students as junior research collaborators. Research grants are often increased in size to cover the additional costs of a student research associate. These add-ons to research grants are called "REU Supplements". In addition, NSF offers funding opportunities to professors at U.S. universities and colleges who want to run inter-university research projects staffed by undergraduates ("REU Sites Awards"). Typically these are partnerships among two or more U.S. universities that bring together groups of at least eight undergraduate students for a summer-long group research project. Two of these REU Site Awards have been international partnerships (with France and the Czech Republic.) NSF is promoting additional international research partnerships under the REU-Sites activity. [7]

INTEGRATED GRADUATE EDUCATION AND RESEARCH TRAINING

Another of NSF's crosscutting programs is the Integrated Graduate Education and Research Training Program. [8] This program builds on one of the great strengths of the U.S. system of higher education – its emphasis on independent research leading to the Ph.D. degree. To encourage interdisciplinarity in this graduate research training experience, NSF created the IGERT Program. IGERT provides five years of support at high levels ($500,000/year) for support of interdisciplinary research training groups. These groups commonly cross departmental boundaries within a university and often involve multiple universities. NSF is very interested in making IGERT a program that supports international collaborations as well.

INSTITUTION-WIDE INTEGRATION OF RESEARCH AND EDUCATION

NSF held two competitions to identify and reward those universities and colleges that were doing the most innovative and effective job of integrating research and education, and to underscore the Foundation's dedication to this practice. These were non-traditional competitions in two respects. First, applications based on past activities and achievements were solicited from the

---

[7]   Program guidelines for the REU Sites activity can be found on the Web at <http://www.nsf.gov/home/crssprgm/reu/start.htm>.

[8]   IGERT: <http://www.nsf.gov/home/crssprgm/igert/start.htm>.

community. This is in stark contrast to NSF's normal calls for proposals that describe future work. Second, applications had to come from the President or Provost of the submitting institution, and only one application per institution was permitted. In this way, NSF sought applications that would describe institution-wide reform efforts that integrate research and education.

Applicants were asked to articulate their vision for the integration of research and education on their campuses, and to identify specific, tangible, measurable indicators of progress toward that vision. They were then asked to provide the data that demonstrated their success.

In 1997, NSF awarded ten research universities Recognition Awards for the Integration of Research and Education (RAIRE). The following year, ten more Awards for the Integration of Research and Education (AIRE) were made to four-year colleges. Their award-winning activities covered a range of issues – curriculum reform, faculty development, hiring and promotion criteria, departmental structure – but they all shared one feature: a clear vision for how integrating research and education improves the quality of both pursuits. Each awardee university or college received $500,000, to be used to expand their program of integration, to evaluate their efforts more formally, and to disseminate information on their activities to other institutions. [9]

AWARD WINNING INSTITUTIONAL PRACTICES

In light of the unusual nature of these two competitions, NSF asked reviewers to provide the Foundation with some 'lessons learned,' some overall observations of what these 20 award-winning institutions had been doing to merit this distinction. They reported that the best applications came from institutions that were re-shaping themselves into student-centered (rather than faculty-centered) universities and colleges. Most commonly, this meant that a large proportion of the faculty were taking students into their labs as co-investigators, not just as lab assistants. This willingness to see students as capable junior colleagues was necessary to winning the award, but it was not sufficient. Putting this attitude into effective practice was a challenge that only the most successful applicants had met.

Virtually all of the institutions that applied had established some sort of research program for undergraduate students. However, at large universities it is extremely difficult to provide more than a small percentage of the students with a true research experience as undergraduates. Successful applicant insti-

---

[9]   Additional information on these competitions and the universities that won them is available on the Web at <http://www.nsf.gov/od/oia/programs/raire/start.htm>.

tutions had used innovative approaches to provide research experiences to a larger portion of their students:

– Establish a research program within the Honors Program and then expand;
– establish a research program for at-risk students and then expand;
– establish a research program for women and underrepresented minorities and then expand; and
– establish a research program for future teachers and then expand.

Many of the successful applicant institutions had realized that a genuine individual research project could not, in practice, be offered to most undergraduate students. These institutions therefore created alternatives to undergraduate research experiences, such as:

– Living/learning/research arrangements for groups of students;
– course-based group research projects;
– inquiry-driven laboratory courses that teach the research process;
– seminars on faculty research;
– work-study programs in industrial research labs;
– problem-based instruction that develop research skills; and
– interactive simulations of experiments on the Web.

To varying degrees, successful applicants had begun the process of changing faculty culture:

– Changing guidelines for hiring, promotion, and/or tenure to create incentives for balancing and integrating research and education;
– creating on-campus centers for improving faculty instruction; and
– creating training and mentoring 'future faculty' programs for graduate students who want to pursue academic careers.

Recipient institutions of the Recognition Awards all had created administrative structures to promote and support various aspects of the integration of research and education. The leadership of these universities had valued the integration of research and education so highly that they committed administrative resources to this function, such as:

– Undergraduate research offices that matched students to faculty mentors;
– funds and offices that offered competitive grants for student research projects;
– centers for courseware development, faculty teaching improvement, and curriculum revision;
– standing committees to promote excellence and innovation in teaching as part of promotion and tenure decisions;

– programs to train graduate students headed for academic careers to use inquiry-based methods and to supervise student research; and

– interdisciplinary and cross-organizational structures that brought education and science faculty together to design courses for future pre- college teachers.

It is interesting to note that even though the public and private research universities were equally represented among the applicants and semi-finalists, only 20% of the RAIRE awardees were private institutions. Reviewers found that the most significant difference between the applications from the two groups was in the area of documentation of results. The public universities had done a much better job of gathering results-oriented data, possibly because they were being held more closely accountable than were private universities. This may have interesting implications for Germany, where nearly all universities are public institutions.

SUMMARY

The two factors that I have discussed today – competition leading to differentiation, and the integration of research and education – are part of the basic culture of U.S. higher education. The resulting landscape of colleges and universities is a very complicated one, and there are significant inefficiencies in the system. Students commonly have to move far from home to attend the school that best fits their needs and goals. Academic careers are extremely insecure in the early stages, and many talented people select other careers for that reason. Even in the later stages of an academic career, many professors elect to change universities in order to find better facilities and more stimulating colleagues.

Integrating research and education also creates inefficiencies. Course content must be continuously updated to incorporate new research findings. Providing students with real research opportunities is more expensive than classroom teaching and adds to the faculty's workload. Teaching methods must evolve in response to new teaching technologies, and new discoveries of how people learn.

For these reasons, the U.S. system of higher education continues to thrive in a competitive, constantly changing landscape. Centers of excellence appear and disappear all the time. Reputations of departments rise and fall. Individual courses come and go, and entire curricula are constantly undergoing reform and improvement. Yet despite its inefficient and unpredictable nature, the U.S.

system of higher education persists as a highly successful and dynamic enterprise.

AMERICAN HIGHER EDUCATION: A MODEL FOR GERMANY? A SKEPTICAL PERSPECTIVE

Horst MEWES

Most participants of the conference documented here agreed about the following claims: 1. The German system of higher education is in need of considerable reform. [1] 2. The American system of higher education (if indeed it constitutes a system) is not as such transferable to German conditions. 3. However, certain alleged characteristics of American higher education often mentioned by German reformers, merit attention. Among these are its flexibility, diversity, and adaptability to rapid change, its innovative capacities, its general accountability to students and society, its dedication to competition for the sake of excellence. It may well be true that compared to the present German university-system some of these features are more characteristic of American higher education. But lest observers become the victims of (potentially very costly) illusions, it pays to also call attention to some general problems facing American higher education frequently ignored by German observers as well as Americans eager to proselytize abroad.

However, one must begin with a reminder of another major theme of the conference, namely that any meaningful reforms of German university-education have been hindered by lack of political (and thus financial) support. It is not clear how under these circumstances any important aspects of the generally very expensive American system can be transferred to Germany. It is well known that the traditional German system of higher education, with its re-

Horst MEWES: Professor of Political Theory and Philosophy at the University of Colorado, Boulder, Member of the University of Colorado Honors Board, and Director of Departmental Honors Program, Political Science; former teaching assignments at the Universität Tübingen and Erlangen; his publications include articles in political theory, books on Thomas Hobbes and Liberalism, on the political system in the U.S., and he has edited a book on Arendt and Strauss.

[1] Whether and to what extent the American system is in need of reforms is a question that deserves some attention, too.

liance upon the Humboldtian ideal of highly independent, individual learning, has been under enormous adverse pressure for several decades. Specifically, it has been forced to operate under the completely perverse conditions of accommodating ever growing numbers of students, while simultaneously absorbing financial cutbacks requiring continuous reduction in human and material resources. It would appear that under such circumstances genuine reforms would be extremely difficult if not impossible.

Nonetheless, the German reform debates over the last decades have focussed in part on measures to a large degree adapted from the U.S. These measures include making German academics more responsive to the teaching needs of a rapidly increasing and changing student body. A related step is linking professional research productivity and teaching loads to the salaries of university professors. The discussion has included debates on the desirability and utility of student tuition for both more student influence on university performance and the university financial independence. Finally, it has focussed on the experimental adoption of the "Anglo-Saxon" BA and MA degrees. The latter is mainly viewed as a convenient measure for certifying the large number of students unable to complete the rigorous traditional university program leading to the doctorate. [2] Reform has not included, however, the widespread founding of (American-style) private universities as an alternative to publicly funded institutions. This despite the pioneering efforts of Konrad Schily and the founding of Witten/Herdecke in 1982. Thus, any German reform measures must take place within the framework of the existing, mainly state-controlled universities. This immediately denies the German system much of the flexibility built into the American mix of private and public institutions.

With this background in mind, it may be useful to a German audience to consider at least *some fundamental aspects* of the current American debate about the state of higher education in America. If that debate shows nothing else, it further underscores the uniqueness of the American system. It also shows the untenable but widely held opinion that while one may not utilize the entire system, one could at least transfer certain parts of American higher education in Germany. For it appears that the *parts* take their function and meaning from the system as a *whole:* if the latter cannot be imitated, neither can its more significant parts. [3] The more systemic problems currently faced by

---

[2]   The 17.000-member-*Deutsche Hochschulverband*, the association of German University teachers, has rejected all of these measures, except tuition. Tuition is rejected by the SPD on political principle.

[3]   The use of the BA and MA degrees at an increasing number of German universities (and its encouragement by a number of state cultural ministries) is a case in point. Using the BA to

the overall *system* of American higher education also show that some of the reform measures, now considered by Germany under very unfavorable financial circumstances, are not entirely unproblematic even under the more favorable conditions currently prevailing in the U.S.

I must limit myself here to three central and interdependent problems associated with American higher education. The first, and perhaps most important, question concerns the success of the American "research universities," the part of the American higher education system most relevant to Germany.[4] The 125 American research universities, a mere 3% of all higher education institutions, have since the late 19th century attempted to combine the German-inspired model of graduate education with the traditional 19th century American institution of *liberal education* identified with the undergraduate college. Has this combination worked satisfactorily? According to a recent, widely circulated report by the prestigious Carnegie Foundation for the Advancement of Teaching, it has not. The *Boyer Report* claims that the state of undergraduate education at research universities is in a state of "crisis," suggesting a record of "failure."[5] The report strongly suggests that the very success of American *graduate* education has led to a failure of *undergraduate* education at these prominent research universities, which grant around 32% of all undergraduate degrees. What if anything can German reformers intent upon adopting the BA degree to fit their university structure learn from this debate?

This alleged "failure" of undergraduate education at research universities raises the second important question concerning American higher education, namely the contemporary condition of the tradition of liberal education in the U.S. The *Boyer Report* identifies 18% or 637 of institutions of higher learning as four-year baccalaureate colleges. In the Winter 1999 issue of *Daedalus* magazine, devoted to the state of liberal education, 212 colleges are identified as the "remaining *residential* liberal arts colleges" of the U.S. In the 1990's, fewer than 250,000 students out of a total of 14 million experience education

---

be "competitive" on an international level by simply awarding it to students with a certain number of semester hours short of the doctorate or state exam does not in any way make it competitive with a genuine BA in the USA or elsewhere. In fact, it would condemn it to an inferior status, compared with a degree awarded in completion of a carefully planned, comprehensive American undergraduate educational program.

[4]   The definition of a "research university " is taken from the Boyer Commission on Educating Undergraduates in the Research University: *Reinventing Undergraduate Education* (Carnegie Foundation for the Advancement of Teaching; no date of publication given, but the Commission has met since 1995), the so-called *Boyer-Report*.

[5]   *Boyer Report* 37.

in a small residential college without graduate students. [6] What, under these conditions, are the purpose, meaning and functions of liberal undergraduate education today? Does higher education in America still revolve around or fundamentally depend upon this "distinctively American" notion of educating "liberal" undergraduates? [7] And if not, what takes its place today? What can the decline of traditional liberal arts education in the U.S. teach Germans about the structure and purpose of entry-level university education with a "mass- audience" of students?

The third and final question I want to raise concerns the overall state and purpose of the *totality* of the American "system" of higher education. It is not widely known even among German educational circles, whether admiring or critical of the "elitism" of American higher education, how highly differentiated and hierarchical this "system" is. It must be emphasized how much the exclusive top-tiers of the university system are favored in terms of financial and other resources over the numerically much larger, but less supported base. Of the approximately 3,500 institutions of higher education, 41% or 1,471 are two-year associate of arts colleges. Nation-wide it is estimated that less than 20% of its students ever continue their studies in four-year institutions. As Prof. Daniel Fallon points out, the California system of higher education is exemplary of the different layers of institutions: the top 12% of high-school graduates (judged by performance) attend nine universities. The next 34% are allowed to attend 22 four-year colleges, and the rest go to the 108 two-year colleges. About 74% of California students in higher education attend these two-year junior colleges, with 18% going to four-year institutions, and about 8% attending universities.

President Clinton in 1997 called attention to the general importance of two-year colleges by claiming an "American birthright" to at least two years of college education. He supported this claim by proposals for special scholarships and tax-credits for middle-income families. [8] The hallmarks of *community colleges* are supposed to be excellence of *teaching* and special emphasis on community- service (including cooperative job-training agreements with private industry). However, these colleges, due mostly to inadequate financial support by communities and state governments, depend in fact upon part- time teachers (adjuncts) for 64% of their teaching staffs. This number is

---

[6]   "Distinctively American: the Residential Liberal Arts Colleges," *Daedalus*, Winter 1999: 49.

[7]   "Distinctively American" 49.

[8]   Quoted in Zachary Karabell, *What's College For? The Struggle To Define American Higher Education* (New York: Basic Books 1998) 213.

predicted to rise to 75% in the early years of the next century. [9] Indeed, within a decade the majority of *all* college teaching in the U.S. will be done by part-time adjuncts, since they already do approximately 1/3 of the teaching even at doctorate-granting universities. Since these adjuncts teach on short-term contracts, are paid by the course, and do not hold permanent, tenured positions, they earn less on average and have less job security than unionized American high school and grade-school teachers. [10] Some expert's claim that 75% of all adjunct college-teachers were they to depend entirely upon their teaching wages would live at or below the official U.S poverty level. [11] And while at the 125 research universities (covering widely diverse institutions ranging from Harvard and Stanford to Mississippi State and Brigham Young universities), more than 70% of professors hold tenure-track positions, at two-year colleges, more than 70% do not have tenure-track jobs. [12]

What can one conclude from these elementary facts about the American system of higher education? For one, it must be understood that although the U.S. is ranked first among nations regarding the percentage (52% as compared to Germany's 27%) of its students attending universities or colleges, the majority of those students attend the most neglected part of American higher education, the two-year junior colleges. [13] The first question German reformers of higher education must answer is where and how the German equivalent of that American student majority is being educated in Germany. Is the broad American differentiation ranging from academically undemanding junior colleges (admitting all applicants) to exclusive research universities the equivalent of German student differential at the pre-collegiate level of education? Does the lower percentage of German students entering higher education at the "research university" level require less qualitative distinctions between those students, and thus their respective institutions of higher education? And, concomitantly, are the gross inequities Americans show in the support of the lower and higher parts of their "system" of higher education advantageous or disad-

---

[9]   Karabell 192, U.S. Dept. of Education figures.

[10] Karabell 206.

[11] Karabell 206.

[12] Karabell 128. Also see John Roueche, Susanne Roueche, and Mark Milliron, *Strangers in Their Own Land: Part-time Faculty in American Community Colleges* (Washington D.C.: Community College Press, 1995); Courtney Leatherman, "Growing Use of Part-Time Professors Prompts Debate and Calls for Action," *Chronicle of Higher Education* (10 October 1997; Edgar Boone, "National Perspective of Community Colleges," *Community College Journal of Research and Practice* vol. 21 (1997).

[13] I note in passing that this also means that the majority of American students pay little if any tuition for their studies.

vantageous to their national educational goals and purpose? Does the American system ranging from junior colleges to highly selective universities amount to a neglect of the democratic majority and a favoring of the already favored upper-middle class? Or, alternatively, does it, in contrast to Germany, signify a broadening and widening of opportunities to those less well prepared and talented? One of the top priorities of German reformers ought to be a study of the relation between American research universities and the extensive system of junior colleges.

Furthermore, what does the Carnegie Foundation's *Boyer Commission Report* on the alleged "crisis" and "failure" of undergraduate education at the level of the American research universities reveal to German reformers? Some German states intend to introduce the BA degree as a terminal degree for an entry-level general studies program, after which a minority of students with appropriate credentials can advance to a graduate-type degree program issuing in a Ph.D. or its equivalent. The *Boyer Report* strongly suggests that this combination has not worked at American research universities. Why and how should it work in Germany? In terms of their "primary responsibility," the "creation and refinement of knowledge," the report concludes that research universities have been "superbly successful." Indeed, they have become the "wellsprings of national stature and achievement." [14] But at the same time, undergraduate education has been grossly neglected. Reform efforts have been "timid, sporadic, limited and unavailing." Universities have shown "complacency and indifference" toward undergraduates, "that constituency whose support is vital to the academic enterprise." [15] Moreover, the *Report* claims that research universities cannot solve their problem by means of "clumsy adaptations of the practices of liberal arts colleges." For research universities, "so complex, so multifaceted, and often so fragmented that, short of major crisis, they can rarely focus their attention on a single agenda," cannot gain their communal identity from outdated notions of liberal education. Instead, "dramatic change" is called for. [16] The *Report's* answer lies in a productive integration of undergraduates into the research processes of the various scientific disciplines. Undergraduates must be turned into productive scholars "articulate and adept in the techniques and

---

[14]   *Boyer Report* 37.

[15]   *Boyer Report* 37.

[16]   It should be noted that changes are already being made. Such prominent institutions as the National Science Foundation have encouraged changes in teaching approaches by awarding grants to the most innovative institutions. See NSF PR 97–10 News of February 11, 1997, which announces ten $ 500,000 three-year grants to ten institutions. 100 out of 137 research-oriented institutions had participated in a competition for these awards.

methods of their chosen fields." [17] In short, the report concludes that under-graduates at research universities must be educated in the manner of graduate students.

But when the *Boyer Report* turns to the education of graduate students at research universities, it gets caught in contradictions undermining the credibility of its entire analysis. For while it wants to treat undergraduates like graduate students, the latter, it turns out, have also been ill served by research universities. Briefly, graduate programs now are designed to produce Ph.D. capable of doing advanced research at other prestigious research universities. But in point of fact, "most" graduate students cannot be expected to find future employment at the 3% of the nation's institutions of higher education that are research universities. Thus, the latter, according to the report, "severely neglects" to prepare most graduate students for their most likely futures, namely their career as *college* professors at small liberal arts colleges, lower-status state universities or even junior colleges. For the year 1994, statistics indicate that 26% of faculty with Ph.D. worked for research universities, 51% worked at four-year colleges, and over 22% worked for two-year colleges. [18] These statistics do not include part-time teachers or adjuncts. Consequently, research universities failed to educate over 73% of its graduates for their main professional activity of college teaching. However, one is forced to ask how this failure can be squared with the *Report's* advice of turning *undergraduate education into a mirror image of the (largely misguided) graduate program.*

This paradox results from the fact that the *Boyer Report* supports the notion that even the 3% of research universities, primarily serving society by virtue of the advancement of knowledge, still have the broader obligation to serve society's need for a comprehensive and more inclusive system of *college* education. But it is suggested, ambiguously, that this task be fulfilled by training teachers for the more broad-based system in the form of *research-teachers.* Critical observers question whether the wider system of higher education is in need of this type of teachers. The inconsistencies of the Carnegie reform model inadvertently raise once again questions about the significance of traditional American *liberal education* for college education other than that of research universities. As we noted above, liberal education as a model for American higher education has been in massive retreat. Originally, this mainly 19th century model of education entailed the creation of an elite of gentlemen and women of liberal mind and disposition. It was a notion of moral and personal

[17] *Boyer Report* 38.
[18] *Boyer Report* 30.

education, the creation of character by means of mental and spiritual exercises of the highest order. [19] Although traditional liberal education was clearly "elitist" in intention, it intended an elite of public leaders for a republican democracy. Its political significance was frequently underscored by viewing liberal education as the highest form of *citizenship* training.

Ironically enough, but perhaps unavoidably, liberal education is more exclusive and "elitist" in our era of "mass-education" than it was during its inception more than a century ago. Not surprisingly, the "212 remaining residential liberal arts colleges" find themselves right in the center of the cross-pressures pervading the entire system of American higher education. Here, the liberal arts tradition meets head-on with the research-orientation of the dominant universities. But the liberal arts College also feels the pressure to become, like community colleges, a training institute for practical skills and preparations for professional life. Liberal arts colleges, more directly than other institutions of higher learning, are forced to choose between becoming a "research college," a smaller (and therefore inferior) version of a research university, or remain a distinctly different liberal arts college. Another option would be to increase useful service to and involvement with the community, thus becoming a grander version of two-year community colleges. [20] But what precisely, or even imprecisely, would a liberal education mean under the circumstances prevailing at the end of the millennium?

Obviously, I cannot do justice here to this complex question. Suffice it to say that generally speaking three answers predominate. As a minimum, a liberal education is said to be "resistant to highly specific vocational preparation and insisting on a considerable breadth of studies." Character formation is still the goal: the "hope that liberal arts colleges will develop interests and capabilities that will enrich both the individual learner and future communities" predominates even today. [21] Another notion of liberal education, more specific than the rather vague one above, focuses on more practical citizenship training. It is suggested that "liberal arts colleges can find new vitality and appeal by adding responsible citizenship as a discrete undergraduate dimension." [22] The

---

[19] I must ignore here the origins of liberal education in the religious origins and affiliations of the oldest American colleges. See Christopher J. Lucas, *American Higher Education: A History* (New York: St. Martin's Griffen, 1994); William C. Ringenberg, *The Christian College: A History of Protestant Higher Education in America* (Grand Rapids: Christian University Press, 1984).

[20] "Distinctively American" 34.

[21] "Distinctively American" 23.

[22] "Distinctively American" 143.

basis of a "philosophy of liberal arts" is the "philosophy of democratic society in which citizenship, social responsibility, and community are inseparable." It is characterized by "an ongoing effort to develop informed, humane, and thoughtful judgments of social issues" and act accordingly. [23] This is a contemporary restatement of the political dimension underlying traditional definitions of American liberal education. Finally, yet another definition of the purpose of liberal education speaks in favor of the adaptation of "the historic function of moral education" to the modern liberal arts college and the society of which it is a part. [24] The goal of liberal education is to be the "conscience of American undergraduate education" by means of moral education, firmly rejecting any imitation of "the research model" and a "general blurring of distinctions" between "residential elite schools" and the "larger institutions." [25] Significantly, this purpose implies that today's pervasive emphasis on diversity is no longer viewed as an institutional or societal goal in itself. Rather, a diversified population is seen as "shaping shared goals to enhance the quality of our common life" both in higher education and in the world around it. [26]

My point is to show that at least in the sphere of small American liberal arts colleges the debate about the meaning and purpose of such liberal education is continuing, if not intensifying. Such education is said to respond to a "felt need of society." [27] Or, alternatively, it is asserted that it could provide "a unique and marketable identity" for liberal education in the highly diversified higher education of contemporary America. However, as such it can no longer provide the standard model of purposive education for the vast majority of American institutions of higher learning. By its own admission, the "purpose" of research universities is, to use the words of the *Boyer Report* once again, as complex, multifaceted and fragmented as the larger society itself. It is, therefore, as incapable of "attention to a single agenda" as is that society. [28] The purpose of research is more research, and the interest of society is research beneficial to society. It is that simple and that complex. In contrast, the citizenship or moral training of liberal education will be restricted to a "privileged" few.

To conclude this brief and sketchy look at a basic incoherence in the over-

---

[23] "Distinctively American" 140.

[24] This is the argument of the highly respected Peter J. Gomes, Professor of Christian Morals and Minister in the Memorial Church at Harvard University. Cf. "Distinctively American" 116.

[25] "Distinctively American" 116.

[26] "Distinctively American" 116.

[27] "Distinctively American" 116.

[28] *Boyer Report* 37.

all "system" of American higher education, we end with two diametrically opposed observations. On the one hand, American higher education has managed to serve the diverse interests of a "highly developed, highly diverse" information society" dependent for its well being and progress upon all forms of marketable and useful knowledge. It is motivated, through the academic professions controlling it, to competition for excellence defined by the prevailing majority consensus of the professions ensconced in the universities. On the whole, it has succeeded in training a growing number of students for a growing field of new skills and professions. However, it is equally true that American higher education is less responsible to societal needs than it is to the self-interest of academic professionals engaged in what frequently amounts to esoteric and career-serving research. Scientific research is (unrealistically) proclaimed the model of most academic fields. [29] Academic professions are unwilling and indeed unable to provide "moral" leadership or educate citizens for a modern democracy. Higher education is not an independent social or cultural force, but simply reflects the multifaceted complexities of a fragmented society. The academic professions of higher education have no responsibility for the overall state of the American system of higher education. These contradictory conclusions are not mutually exclusive. The growing complexities of a "knowledge society" have issued in an equally complex system of higher education, consisting not only of "modern" research universities, but in part of the historical accretion of various institutionalized traditions and customs (ranging from religious colleges to land-grant agricultural colleges).

From the point of view of national educational policy and long-range national interest, the partial, undeniable success of American higher education has created problems of its own. The American strongly hierarchical system has not prevented, and perhaps has exacerbated, the decline of quality, both among students and faculty, in much of the system immediately below the top institutions. The leaders of academic professions neither know nor care about the conditions of the "system" of higher education, increasingly leaving such matters to professional administrators or experts on education. Paradoxically, German professors, looking at the deteriorating condition of perhaps most of the teachers in American higher education, are wise to insist upon protecting their valuable traditional independence. However, they are entirely wrong, and ultimately self-destructive, in doing so without taking on greater responsibility for the reform of what ought to be *their* universities. In this, German

---

[29] And in those disciplines where there are other models, they often are, as in the case of various ideologies of "post-modernism," the reflection of esoteric academic trends.

and American academic professionals have more in common than they realize. German reformers could do no worse than to adapt those aspects of the (inadequate) American system, which would further reduce the responsibilities of the German professorate.

If not higher education itself, modern democratic society does require broad-based, quality education. A purely elitist form of higher education, if it does not serve to imbue the *entire "system"* with the principles of excellence and responsibility, will ultimately develop its own forms of pathology and contribute, even if inadvertently, to the weakening of highly complex, modern democracy. Politicians, unable to understand the many cross-pressures operating within universities, are unlikely to offer genuine improvements.

WHAT CAN THE TWO SYSTEMS LEARN FROM ONE ANOTHER?

Wedigo DE VIVANCO

CURRENT SITUATION

The system of higher education in the United States is completely individual-ized. Individual colleges and universities – depending on one's definition, there are between 3,600 and 6,000 – act highly autonomously. Even the state universities usually get much less than 50% of their budget from public sources, in many cases even as little as 20%. The remaining funds are made up from student fees, outside sources, and donations. The less public money flowing into the institution, the less government control plays a part in its operation. This does not affect the duty to report on and render account of outside sources of funding.

In Germany, however, everything is ruled by a high degree of dependency on the government, on the one hand financially –usually over 90% of the budget is government money –, on the other hand, there is the strict regimentation by the *Hochschulrahmengesetz* (Federal Law) and the *Landeshochschulgesetze* (State Laws) as well as by the governmental bureaucracies. The development toward greater autonomy in the universities and the granting of global budgets is very recent. In Germany, there is also considerable fund-raising from outside sources, but there are no revenues from student fees (with very few exceptions) and only a negligible financial support of the colleges through donations.

The two systems are the results of the two very different cultures which have manifested themselves in the different forms of the individual universities, particularly in the day-to-day running of the institution. To emphasize this

Wedigo DE VIVANCO: Dean of International Affairs at the Freie Universität Berlin, holding memberships of the Advisory Council for New Programs of the German Academic Exchange Service (DAAD), the Executive Board of the European Association of International Education (EAIE), and of the Training Committee of the EAIE; former head of the DAAD office in New York, Professor for German Studies at New York University, Lecturer for German History at the University of London, and Personal Assistant to the Vice President at the Freie Universität Berlin.

thesis, I would like to refer to the basic differences of the governments' role in society. Here in Germany, the government is generally regarded as a mediator between various interests and as fair distributor of the Gross National Product. Through taxation, the government can provide a socially fair infrastructure and balance extreme differences. In the United States, government involvement is avoided and there is a consensus among the population to reduce government to an absolute minimum. In other words, the government has very little means to reallocate funds and to contribute to social equality. The belief in the market and the moral duty of private philanthropy is strong and consequently these are the generally accepted sources for the redistribution of the Gross National Product.

A comparison between these two systems can help remove existing prejudices or half-knowledge as the other contributions have demonstrated. For example, an argument which has been raised again and again, that there are no permanent positions in the United States, is utterly false and even if one looks carefully, untenable. On the contrary, as a consequence of the recent anti-discrimination policy there is the great problem that there is no longer an age of compulsory retirement. Instead, individual university employees can decide when they would like to retire. It is obvious that this will form a heavy burden for any planning by the university administration.

WHAT CAN THE UNITED STATES LEARN FROM GERMANY?

Unfortunately, there is not much to mention here since the United States has learned quite a lot from the German university system in the nineteenth century. For example it has introduced Humboldt's dualistic concept of the integration of research and learning and the tendency to keep the predominant part of research in the university and not to have it done at specifically created research institutes.

However, it is a result of an exemplary German policy that basic research receives more publicly financed support than in the United States. On the one hand, this is the effect of different concepts of long-range planning, which in the US means five years, while in Germany, five years would be the basis of a medium-length budget plan. Consequently, in Germany there is much more long-term investment in basic research. Unquestionably, this is something the United States can learn from.

Another considerable advantage of our system of education is that early on in their lives, the self-determination of the students is supported and required. The fact that this aspect has come into question has been made evident by the increasingly strong demand that courses of study should be given more structure and to move in the direction of guided education. Nevertheless, studying in Germany, being much more liberal, autonomous and led by one's own curiosity and one's own interests, contributes to an earlier academic independence which is essential for the definition of new areas of research. This kind of academic independence is usually found in American universities only after graduation (B.A.).

WHAT CAN WE LEARN FROM THE AMERICANS?

There is a lot of which I will only mention a few essential elements which have also been addressed in the previous papers. As my report is to be a kind of a summary, I should like to comment upon the following central aspects:

1. The great autonomy of the American system of universities and colleges has big advantages which concern the flexibility of the education market, clarification of goals, and placement in the area of education. In addition to these public aspects, a high level of autonomy has the great advantage that internally, the available resources can be more goal-directed. The institution itself can decide in which "league" it wants to play. This makes sense on many levels. Some of the most important I would like to put in key words: The accreditation by professional organizations which define an agreed upon minimum standard for membership, entails among other things minimum requirements concerning academic standing and character qualities of the students; the ability to finance the colleges and universities through outside sources, sponsoring and alumni funds as well as student tuition; the assets of the faculty, the quality of research, but also evaluation and accreditation.

2. As a strength of the American system, I consider the openly admitted differentiation according to rankings. To be true, this has existed covertly in Germany for a long time. That is, a German personnel manager will not necessarily be influenced by the name of a university, but he will pay attention to by whom and at what institute the applicant has studied when he wants to hire him for a particular job. The claim that in Germany all university diplomas are weighed equally seems to me to be a popular myth than factual reality. Personnel managers employ applicants according to differentiated criteria. The advantage of the openly differentiated system lies in the fact that an institution will be more easily aware of its weaknesses and strengths and can set forth its institutional policies with that in mind. I think the presidents of universities will try to establish and build up their

strengths, and after repeated attempts, they will possibly get rid of the weakest sections. That does not mean that institutions will not retain the happy medium, but that they will do so with an eye on bringing about an improvement in quality in these areas as well. A differentiation of the university system of this nature will go hand in hand with a considerable differentiation in the student body. In other words, the strongest institutions will get the most gifted and talented students and accept to be challenged by these, which means these students must also have the best teachers.

3. A clear strength of the American system of colleges and universities is the system of degrees. We Germans should adopt the three-tier structure of Bachelor of Arts (B.A.), Master (M.A.) and Dr. (Ph.D.) in any case. In my opinion, this system has only advantages and would revolutionize the system of the Federal Republic; not only because we would be more compatible on the international academic market, but because at the same time we would gain a meaningful differentiation of the student body. What is key is that in a system like this credit points and equivalent transfer credits would be calculated as is also stipulated by the ECTS (European Credit Transfer System) which is being introduced at the moment. Most important here is an additional aspect, namely the cumulative grade. The final exam should no longer determine the success or failure of a course of study. Instead, the cumulative work of the student will be considered. This would lead to the GPA (grade point average) system which is used in the US. This system motivates the student from his first semester on to completely concentrate on all his courses, as he knows that the results of each course will influence his final cumulative grade. It goes without saying that the grades would be weighed differently. One large advantage of records of grades and credits accompanying the course of studies is that its length would be considerably shortened. In addition, the student in such a gradated system would have a better understanding of his ability right from the beginning. In this way, the Bachelor's degree will provide the first proof of the academic ability of a student and at the same time qualify him for many positions in the labor market, but it will also provide the above average student with the requirement for further studies. This will enable the universities to be far more selective in the admission of Master (Magister) students and to create more homogeneous groups who could better inspire each other. For this degree, too, the cumulative grade and the credit point system is to be applied, which will make it easier to change to another course of study as well as keep up the level of motivation for the student to concentrate fully on his current

course of study. After the granting of the master's degree, those particularly gifted students can apply for the courses leading to the Ph.D. This would be the advanced graduate studies which on some level already exist in the *Graduiertenkollegs* or in the institutions of research outside the university with representatives of the S-professorships.

Increasingly, a new category of master's studies will be introduced that is less a simple continuation of the academic career after the Bachelor's degree, but is intended to cover a certain professional profile, for example the existing degree of Master of Business Administration, Master of Public Health etc. These are professional courses of study which address individuals with some years of professional experience. In other words, a broadening of the structure of the system of studies in more degrees would serve the ever-growing future necessity of lifelong learning. To keep up with the competition, people will need to acquire additional academic qualifications at different stages of their lives. These should not only be offered by private institutions, but should be especially offered by the universities. Germany should also adopt the widespread American practice where further professional training is rewarded with salary increases as a reward for personal initiative.

4. German universities can learn a lot from the selectivity of the American system of college entrance. Clearly this defines the identity of the colleges and universities through the admission of individual students. The educational institutions compete for the students who best fit them. Therefore, in the long run, German universities should pay more attention to the admission of individual students, and not only schematically consider the Abitur-grade or the ZVS (central allotment of university admissions) distribution system in Dortmund. The students are the most important and most significant capital for securing the future the universities have. Therefore, it is also necessary that each student is taken seriously as an individual and is admitted with an aim in mind. The previously described gradated degree system has the advantage that at each of the respective stages the most suitable students could be admitted. This will lead to more efficiency and a better comparison of the individual students in the respective courses of study.

5. The above would imply the introduction of student fees. Under the condition that Germany would provide a fair system of grants and loans accessible for each citizen, the universities should be allowed to charge fees. This has several advantages. On the one hand the budget of the university will be less dependent upon the state parliament. Furthermore, it will improve the

internal performance of the universities. The fees, especially the individual fees raised by a given university, will enable one to better estimate the market value of a university. In the end, students will reveal where they would like to study simply by showing up. This is of course subject to a fair system of loans and grants. Tuition will certainly result in more discipline among the students. In other words, they will put more effort into trying to finish their studies within the stipulated time in order not to incur additional costs by additional terms. Also, one can expect that when students are charged with their own financial contribution to their college, they will identify with it to a greater extent. This would especially have a positive influence on their treatment of the university's facilities such as rooms, books, furniture, bathrooms, green areas, etc. Student fees will make students more clearly into customers, thus obliging the universities to provide better services. He who does not respond sufficiently to the needs of the paying students will lose them to the competition.

6. Closely related to the introduction of tuition fees there are the often excellent models of performance-oriented allocations of funds at American universities. Through the last years in Germany the question of how such funds could be fairly allocated has been rigorously discussed. It would be essential to connect the salary system with the system of allocating funds. In addition to the mere distribution of infrastructure and research funds, the employees at the university should be paid according to their performance. There are a number of American universities from which we can learn and adopt various practices.

7. At American universities, cooperation with the alumni is exemplary. Here, German universities have barely, if at all, begun to be active. The alumni, that is, the graduates of a university, are one of the best ways to secure the future of a university. As yet, German universities have not been successful in establishing strong ties between the alumni and their Alma Mater. Mainly this is because the graduates don't identify with the latter. They take it for granted that the government has to provide talented young people with a university. Students only realize the fact that the institution has contributed considerably to their professional success after they have finished half of their working life. At that point the distance from the *alma mater* is usually too great for reestablishing their connection to it. German universities should make use of the experience of centuries of American universities and find a way to stay in touch with former students which has been adapted to German culture. Alumni should not only be seen as "cash cows" to pad

continuously shrinking university budgets, but as friends and supporters in a political and professional context. This especially entails providing internships and jobs for the graduates.

8. Grantwriting is especially attractive at American universities as outside sources can usually also cover so-called overhead costs. In other words, funds which are donated to a particular research project help finance the infrastructure of the whole university to a considerable extent. Especially those academic branches which usually do not have access to sufficient outside funding profit from this. These branches can thus be financed and supported in their high-quality work. The overhead need not necessarily amount to such excessive sums as can be found at some research intensive universities in the US. However, it should alleviate the costs of the infrastructure considerably. For example, at Stanford University and other research intensive universities, for every dollar collected from outside sources, 70 cents go to the overhead of running the administration. This is also due to the fact that this overhead includes both building investment and costs of operations. In Germany, we would move a considerable step forward if outsourced funds of the *Deutsche Forschungsgemeinschaft* would include an overhead of between 10 and 30 percent.

Let me summarize: Germans can learn a lot from the American system of higher education. However, I would like to add warningly that the single components we consider worth adopting should not be copied uncritically. Instead, we should thoroughly think about the resulting consequences for our system and be aware of them. As you might have noticed, I am a strong supporter of a more performance and market-oriented university system. This implies that we need to introduce student fees, that our salaries will be more performancé-oriented, that the admission of students is exclusively up to the universities, and eventually, that we have to accept a performance-oriented diversification of the German university system.

Publikationen der Bayerischen Amerika-Akademie

Helmbrecht Breinig; Jürgen Gebhardt; Berndt Ostendorf (Hrsg.)
Das deutsche und das amerikanische Hochschulsystem
Bildungskonzepte und Wissenschaftspolitik
Bd. 1, Herbst 2001, 200 S., 48,80 DM, br.,
ISBN 3-8258-4942-2

Studien zu Geschichte, Politik und Gesellschaft Nordamerikas
Studies in North American History, Politics and Society

herausgegeben von
Willi Paul Adams und Knud Krakau
(John F. Kennedy-Institut für Nordamerikastudien, Freie Universität Berlin)
Norbert Finzsch (Universität Hamburg)
und Rolf Meyn (Universität Rostock)

Barbara Held
Die Hispanische Presse in Kalifornien 1955 – 1985
Ethnische Medien als Spiegel und Motor im Assimilationsprozeß US-amerikanischer Minderheiten
Bd. 2, 1997, 408 S., 68,80 DM, br., ISBN 3-8258-3050-0

Susanne Janssen
Vom Zarenreich in den amerikanischen Westen: Deutsche in Rußland und Rußlanddeutsche in den USA (1871 – 1928)
Die politische, sozio-ökonomische und kulturelle Adaptation einer ethnischen Gruppe im Kontext zweier Staaten
Bd. 3, 1997, 344 S., 48,80 DM, br., ISBN 3-8258-3292-9

Michael Behnen
Die USA und Italien 1921 – 1933
Diese Monographie stellt die Beziehungen zwischen den USA und dem faschistischen Italien in den 1920er Jahren und während der Weltwirtschaftskrise auf politischem, finanziellem und wirtschaftlichem Gebiet in einen multinationalen Zusammenhang. Die übergreifende Perspektive ist gegeben durch die Stichworte Kriegsschulden-Abkommen / Währungsstabilisierung / wirtschaftlicher Aufschwung, die einem politischen Isolationismus entgegenstanden.
Der Band schildert die z. T. begeisterte Zustimmung verschiedener Teile der amerikanischen Gesellschaft zum faschistischen System. Führende Banken, vor allem der Ostküste, deckten große Teile des Kapitalbedarfs der italienischen Regierung, der Kommunen und der industriellen Wachstumsbranchen. Sie trugen damit erheblich zur Modernisierung des faschistischen Staates bei. Amerikanische und italienische Staatsmänner kooperierten auf internationalen Konferenzen mit dem Ziel, die Abrüstung zu verhindern und ungehindert in Übereinstimmung mit der Rüstungslobby die nationale Aufrüstung voranzutreiben. Insbesondere zeigt die Benutzung der Archive der amerikanischen, britischen, französischen und italienischen Zentralbanken, in welch enger Weise das System Mussolini mit den finanziellen und wirtschaftlichen, mit den Handels- und Rüstungsinteressen der demokratischen Großmächte beiderseits des Atlantiks verflochten war.
Bd. 4 (2 Bde.), 1999, 800 S., 98,80 DM, br., ISBN 3-8258-3450-6

Gabriele Heidenfelder
From Duppel to Truman Plaza
Die *Berlin American Community* in den Jahren 1965 bis 1989
Die Luftbrücke als Bindeglied zwischen der Geschichte Berlins und der USA und ihrer Streitkräfte ist in diesem Jahr in aller Munde. Eine Verbindung der amerikanischen Soldaten und ihrer Familien zur Bevölkerung Berlins fehlte jedoch weitgehend: Die amerikanischen Streitkräfte in Berlin hatten ihre eigene Geschichte, sie lebten ihr Alltagsleben separat von ihrer Umgebung. Die Regeln, die das Leben und die Rolle dieser Community bestimmten, folgten bestimmten politischen und militärischen Vorgaben. Diese Vorgaben werden hier erstmals untersucht und beschrieben. Die Studie beschäftigt sich in erster Linie intensiv mit der Community selbst. Die vorliegende Arbeit ist das Ergebnis intensiver Recherche. Sowohl die Medien der Community als auch Interviews mit ehemaligen Community-Mitgliedern wurden ausgewertet. Beides liefert reichhaltiges Material zur Erhellung der Prozesse innerhalb der Community. Wichtige Informationen zur US-Armee, speziell in Berlin, bietet darüber hinaus der umfangreiche Anhang.
Bd. 5, 1998, 176 S., 38,80 DM, br., ISBN 3-8258-3270-8

Martin Gehlen
Das amerikanische Sozialnetz im Umbruch
Die Welfare-Reform von 1996 aus europäischer Perspektive
Bd. 6, 1997, 272 S., 49,80 DM, br., ISBN 3-8258-3477-8

LIT Verlag Münster – Hamburg – London
Bestellungen über:
Grevener Str. 179 48159 Münster
Tel.: 0251 – 23 50 91 – Fax: 0251 – 23 19 72
e-Mail: lit@lit-verlag.de – http://www.lit-verlag.de

Preise: unv. PE

Carmen Müller
Weimar im Blick der USA
Amerikanische Auslandskorrespondenten und
Öffentliche Meinung zwischen Perzeption
und Realität
Bd. 7, 1997, 536 S., 59,80 DM, br., ISBN 3-8258-3560-x

Stephan Wolf
Abraham Yates, Jr.
Vergessener Gründervater der amerikanischen
Republik
Bd. 8, 1998, 448 S., 59,80 DM, br., ISBN 3-8258-3603-7

Marion Breunig
**Die Amerikanische Revolution als
Bürgerkrieg**
Aus heutiger Perspektive wird die Amerikanische
Revolution vielfach nur als Unabhängigkeitskrieg
der Kolonien gegen das britische Mutterland wahr-
genommen. Dies ist vor allem das Verdienst der
revolutionären Founding Fathers, denen es gelang,
sich mit ihrer Version der Revolution als einmü-
tiger Erhebung der Amerikaner gegen die engli-
schen Unterdrückungsversuche durchzusetzen. Die
Gründungsmythen der USA verschweigen jedoch
die Existenz einer beachtlichen Opposition zur
Unabhängigkeit. Zwischen 100.000 und 150.000
Menschen haben im Verlauf des Krieges das Land
verlassen; bis zu 50.000 Amerikaner kämpften
während des Kriegs auf britischer Seite. Der
Kampf mit dieser inneren Opposition nahm einen
weitaus größeren Raum ein als weithin bekannt.
Ein engmaschiges Netz revolutionärer Kontroll-
und Sicherheitskomitees diente ausschließlich der
Einschüchterung der neutralen Mehrheit und der
Bestrafung der Gegner. Ziel dieses Buches ist es,
zunächst den schwierigen Entscheidungsprozeß,
dem sich die Kolonisten stellen mußten, transparent zu machen und sodann zu zeigen, in welch
hohem Maße der Revolutionskrieg ein Bürgerkrieg
war.
Bd. 9, 1998, 376 S., 59,80 DM, br., ISBN 3-8258-3862-5

Michael Löffler
**Preußens und Sachsens Beziehungen zu
den USA während des Sezessionskrieges
1860 – 1865**
Der Sezessionskrieg in den Vereinigten Staaten
von Amerika bildet wahrscheinlich den gravie-
rendsten Einschnitt in der Landesgeschichte, der
aber auch internationale Folgen hervorrief. Die
vorliegende Arbeit klärt, welche Stellung und
welchen Anteil bei der Lösung dieses Konfliktes
Preußen und Sachsen genommen haben. Dabei
wird unterschieden zwischen der aktiven Beteili-
gung auf nördlicher und südlicher Seite und eben-
so zwischen Äußerungen von Angehörigen oder

Beauftragten der preußischen bzw. sächsischen
Länderregierung und privaten Stellungnahmen,
sowie dem Spiegelbild der Geschehnisse in der
Presse.
Bd. 10, 1999, 368 S., 59,80 DM, br., ISBN 3-8258-4185-5

Ute Schwabe
**Moralische Verpflichtung – Strategischer
Vorteil**
Amerikanisch-Israelische Beziehungen nach
Ende des Yom-Kippur-Krieges (1973) bis zur
Unterzeichnung der Declaration of Principles
(1993)
Das besondere Verhältnis zwischen den Vereinigten Staaten und Israel gibt Anlaß zu zahlreichen
Interpretationen. Die Vereinigten Staaten haben
sich seit der Gründung Israels immer für die Existenz des Staates und sein Überleben eingesetzt.
Stets betonten amerikanische Staatsmänner ein
moral commitment der Supermacht gegenüber Israel; aber auch strategische Interessen lassen sich
nicht von der Hand weisen. Die finanzielle Hilfe
an Israel durch die USA – verstärkt seit Ende
der 60er Jahre – wird häufig der Lobbytätigkeit
des *American Israel Public Affairs Committee*
(AIPAC) zugeschrieben, einer Interessengrup-
pe, die sich kontinuierlich für die Verbesserung
des Verhältnisses zwischen Israel und den USA
einsetzt. Es gilt die Rolle von AIPAC im außen-
politischen Entscheidungsprozeß der USA zu
untersuchen: Wie gelingt es der Lobby, sich Ge-
hör zu verschaffen, wie hätte sich die Beziehung
zwischen Israel und den USA ohne die engagierte
Lobby entwickelt? Die Arbeit beleuchtet hier-
bei den direkten Zusammenhang zwischen der
Wirkungsweise von AIPAC und der moralischen
Verpflichtung sowie dem strategischen Interesse
der USA.
Bd. 11, 1999, 320 S., 48,80 DM, br., ISBN 3-8258-4202-9

Katrin Pickenhan
**Glaube und Gesellschaft im Zeitalter der
Aufklärung**
Eine vergleichende Studie zu Massachusetts
und Württemberg im 18. Jahrhundert am Beispiel von Isaac Backus und Magnus Friedrich
Roos
Die Erweckungsbewegungen in den nordameri-
kanischen Kolonien und der Pietismus in Württemberg – zwei frühmoderne Reaktionen des
Protestantismus auf Wandlungsprozesse des 17.
und 18. Jahrhunderts, die große Gemeinsamkeiten
aufweisen.
Warum aber blieb der Pietismus in Württemberg
eine überwiegend innerkirchliche Bewegung, während in Neuengland ein Großteil der Erweckungen
zur Abtrennung von der kongregationalistischen

LIT Verlag Münster – Hamburg – London
Bestellungen über:
Grevener Str. 179 48159 Münster
Tel.: 0251 – 23 50 91 – Fax: 0251 – 23 19 72
e-Mail: lit@lit-verlag.de – http://www.lit-verlag.de
Preise: unv. PE

Kirche und zu Neugründungen evangelikaler Kirchengemeinden führte? Warum stellte sich das Verhältnis zur Obrigkeit und zur Aufklärung so unterschiedlich dar, wenn sich doch die Analyse des "ungläubigen" Zeitalters, in dem man lebte, ähnelte? Die vergleichende Untersuchung verdeutlicht präziser, als dies in Einzelstudien möglich wäre, daß die tieferen Ursachen für die gegensätzliche Entwicklung nicht primär in den unterschiedlichen theologischen Traditionen von Luthertum und Calvinismus gesucht werden sollten. Vielmehr setzten die konkreten politischen und sozialen Bedingungen den entscheidenden Rahmen, innerhalb dessen die Vertreter der religiösen Erneuerungsbewegungen strategische und grundsätzliche Entscheidungen treffen konnten und mußten.

Bd. 12, 1999, 272 S., 48,80 DM, br., ISBN 3-8258-4210-x

Astrid M. Eckert
Feindbilder im Wandel: Ein Vergleich des Deutschland- und des Japanbildes in den USA 1945 und 1946
Am Ende des Zweiten Weltkrieges fielen die amerikanischen Prognosen über die Zukunft der gerade besiegten Staaten düster aus: Mindestens dreißig Jahre müssten Deutschland und Japan unter alliierter Kontrolle bleiben, wollte man sie von einer erneuten Aufrüstung für den Kampf um die Weltmacht abhalten. Stattdessen wurden die ehemaligen Kriegsgegner in einer neuen Mächtekonstellation bald zu Verbündeten der USA. Was aber wurde aus den virulenten Feindbildern der Kriegszeit? Die vorliegende Studie verfolgt die Darstellung Deutschlands und Japans in amerikanischen Zeitschriften durch das letzte Kriegsjahr und die unmittelbare Nachkriegszeit. Sie zeigt den Wandel dieser Feindbilder auf und setzt ihn in Beziehung zu militärischen Entwicklungen, propagandapolitischen Vorgaben, Arbeitsbedingungen von Kriegskorrespondenten und redaktionellen Entscheidungen bei einzelnen Zeitschriften. Besondere Aufmerksamkeit gilt dabei den Spannungen zwischen den zum Teil bewußt geschürten Stimmungen der Kriegszeit und ersten Versuchen, diese wieder zu dämpfen und in neue Richtungen zu lenken.

Bd. 13, 1999, 216 S., 48,80 DM, br., ISBN 3-8258-4211-8

Manfred Berg; Michaela Hönicke;
Raimund Lammersdorf;
Anneke de Rudder (Hrsg.)
Macht und Moral
Beiträge zur Ideologie und Praxis amerikanischer Außenpolitik im 20. Jahrhundert.
Festschrift für Knud Krakau zu seinem 65. Geburtstag
Die Außenpolitik der USA gründet sich auf den Anspruch moralischer Überlegenheit. Doch ist amerikanische Machtausübung im 20. Jahrhundert wirklich Ausdruck demokratischer Moral? Verbirgt sich hinter dem vermeintlich idealistischen Interventionismus nicht doch der Zynismus einer verschworenen Machtelite? Die Autoren des Bandes analysieren diese Fragen vor dem Hintergrund amerikanischer demokratischer Traditionen. Ihre Fallstudien verdeutlichen, daß die Spannung zwischen Macht und Moral in einer Republik ein aktuelles Thema bleibt, dem sich nicht nur die amerikanische Außenpolitik stellen muß.

Bd. 14, 1999, 328 S., 59,80 DM, br., ISBN 3-8258-4302-5

Michaela Hampf
Freies Radio in den USA: Die Pacifica-Foundation, 1946 – 1965
"Freies Radio in den USA: Die Pacifica Foundation, 1946 – 1965" ist eine Geschichte des ältesten und bis heute einzigen unabhängigen und nichtkommerziellen Radionetzwerks der Vereinigten Staaten. KPFA, Pacificas Flagschiff, wurde 1949 von Pazifisten und Pazifistinnen in der San Francisco Bay Area gegründet. Sie vertraten zunächst einen radikal dialogorientierten Ansatz, der sich in den fünfziger und sechziger Jahren mit der Gründung der Schwesterstationen in New York, Los Angeles und Washington unter den Bedingungen des späten McCarthyismus in einen radikal individuellen Free Speech-Ansatz wandelte. Seit über fünfzig Jahren setzt Pacifica sozialem und politischem Konformismus ihre unkonventionellen, oft provokativen und couragierten Programme entgegen. Free Speech von Round-Table Diskussionen zu Free Form Radio – die mittlerweile fünf Sender Pacificas erprobten eine Reihe von innovativen Formaten und inhaltlichen Neuorientierungen, von denen sowohl public und community radio stations als auch die kommerzielle Medienlandschaft bis heute profitieren. Das Buch beleuchtet die Geschichte Pacificas, die bis auf den heutigen Tag als Modell für freies, durch HörerInnen finanziertes Radio auch in Deutschland gelten kann. Gerade auch für deutsche Leserinnen und Leser vermittelt es darüber hinaus Einblicke in die Genese des amerikanischen Rundfunksystems sowie die politischen, technologischen und sozio-kulturellen Faktoren, die Pacificas Entwicklung im Klima des Kalten Kriegs prägten.

Bd. 15, 2000, 216 S., 39,80 DM, br., ISBN 3-8258-4963-5

LIT Verlag Münster – Hamburg – London
Bestellungen über:
Grevener Str. 179 48159 Münster
Tel.: 0251 – 23 50 91 – Fax: 0251 – 23 19 72
e-Mail: lit@lit-verlag.de – http://www.lit-verlag.de
Preise: unv. PE